Jaime Gil de Biedma

Longing

selected poems

Translated from the Spanish by
James Nolan

City Lights

San Francisco

LONGING: SELECTED POEMS
Las personas del verbo: first published by Seix Barral, Barcelona
© 1975, 1982 by Jaime Gil de Biedma
Translation © 1993 by James Nolan

Back cover photograph of Gil de Biedma by Colita Fotografía
Frontispiece: Jaime Gil de Biedma in Manila, 1956.
Cover design by Rex Ray
Typesetting by Harvest Graphics

Several of these translations appeared in *New Laurel Review*.

Library of Congress Cataloging-in-Publication Data

Gil de Biedma, Jaime, 1929-
    Longing : selected poems / by Jaime Gil de Biedma ; translated
from the Spanish by James Nolan.
       p.   cm.
    ISBN 0-87286-277-1 : $9.95
    1. Gil de Biedma, Jaime, 1929-   — Translations into English.

I. Nolan, James, 1947- . II. Title.
PQ6613.I3916.A26   1993
861'.64 — dc20   93-21775
                                        CIP

City Lights Books are available to bookstores through our primary distributor:
Subterranean Company. P. O. Box 160, 265 S. 5th St., Monroe, OR 97456.
503-847-5274. Toll-free orders 800-274-7826. FAX 503-847-6018.
Our books are also available through library jobbers and regional distributors.
For personal orders and catalogs, please write to City Lights Books,
261 Columbus Avenue, San Francisco, CA 94133.

CITY LIGHTS BOOKS are edited by Lawrence Ferlinghetti and Nancy J. Peters and
published at the City Lights Bookstore, 261 Columbus Avenue, San Francisco, CA 94133.

TRANSLATOR'S ACKNOWLEDGMENTS

For their helpful readings of this translation I would like to thank Shirley Mangini, Alonso Carnicer, Juan Ferrate, Mario Lucarda, Susan Ballyn, José Luis Regojo and my editors, Lawrence Ferlinghetti and Nancy J. Peters. I also acknowledge with gratitude the support of the Fulbright Commission in Spain during several teaching fellowships. This book is a belated thank you to Nieves Samblancat and Pere Rovira, who at one time not only gave me their apartment in Barcelona but their favorite poet, Gil de Biedma. The translation is dedicated to Sebastián Camps, who suggested it years ago in the garden of his Casa de las Margaritas in Lloret, Mallorca: "Yo pienso / en cómo ha pasado el tiempo, / y te recuerdo así."

INTRODUCTION: Poetry Under Curfew

Americans may be struck by two wildly contradictory images of modern Spain: a gypsy talking to the moon in a García Lorca poem and, skipping a generation, the espresso-pot earrings dangling from María Brancano in Pedro Almodóvar's film *Women On the Verge of a Nervous Breakdown*. This dramatic transition from the rural gypsy mythology of García Lorca to the wacky urban libido of Almodóvar crosses the desert of the Franco dictatorship. Despite the popularity of Spanish poetry, little is known here of the post-Civil War poets, who chart this painful course from defeated idealism to ironic postmodernism. The foremost poet of this era, Jaime Gil de Biedma, leader of the "Barcelona school," has become a cult figure in contemporary Spain since he died of AIDS in 1990. His poetry and legend help to explain who the Spanish have become and how they survived when, for almost half a century, the lights went out.

The first edition of Gil de Biedma's selected poems wound up, as might be expected, in boxes in the publisher's basement, censored by the government. His life and literary career were bracketed almost entirely by the rise and fall of Generalissimo Francisco Franco, notorious for the suppression of literature. Born in 1929, Gil de Biedma was six years old when García Lorca was murdered in Granada at the outbreak of the Civil War, and his collected poems, *Las personas del verbo*, first appeared in 1975, the year Franco died. What is surprising is that Gil de Biedma was a leftist, homosexual poet from the Catalan capitol, Barcelona — all of Franco's favorite things — who not only published books of autobiographical poetry in Spain but was known as a poet of social conscience as well as erotic lyricism. Like other Spanish poets of his time, he chose his words carefully.

Gil de Biedma is the most original and influential among the poets known as the '50's Generation. In a poem of that decade, "In Luna Castle," he addresses a political prisoner just released from Franco's prison. The long years behind bars are a "gorge separating / those moments from these . . . a chasm in your spirit / you can never bridge." This chasm between the revolutionary ferment before the Civil War and the police-state that followed is as abrupt as the war itself, and as broad and deep as the ensuing industrialization of Spain and the exodus from countryside to city. The poetry of the previous generation — of García Lorca and Rafael Alberti — was an expansion of the romantic imagination, a passionate poetry with a magical sense of language. Although socially committed, this poetry was on the whole rural, an oral poetry as memorable for semiliterate listeners as for educated readers. The ravaged landscape after the Civil War did again produce poetry, although it is as different from that of the Generation of '27 as if it came from another country.

Children during the Civil War, Gil de Biedma's generation was an orphaned one. Their cultural parents were either killed, exiled or imprisoned, and the Spain of their youth was the gray impoverished city dominated by curfews, shortages and censorship. But the loss that most affected these poets is what George Orwell sees as the ultimate result of totalitarianism: the destruction of the national language. Public language was corrupted not only by Franco's control of the media, education, and religion but also of the connotations of words themselves. *Dios* no longer meant God, *Familia* was not my family or yours, and *Patria* was not where the Spanish lived.

What Ignacio Silone writes about Fascist Italy was equally true in Fascist Spain: "He who speaks, lies."

Gil de Biedma subverted the lie of the very language in which he wrote with irony, parody, and humor, weathering out an exile-at-home with cunning. He substituted a liberating cosmopolitanism for the loss of his own culture, and what he gained was to join the larger tradition of 20th-century European poetry. For his generation foreign culture was a crack of light under a bolted door: A trip to Paris, books from London meant everything to him coming of age as a poet. His greatest influences were not only Luis Cernuda and Jorge Guillén but also French Symbolist and Anglo-American poets. Eliot and Auden especially are echoed in his poetry in the soft-spoken conversational voice, the recyling of foreign sources and the undermining of old poetic rhetorics. Often Gil de Biedma's words fall into place in English translation as if coming home to the source of their inspiration.

After a generation of forced isolation, the main anxiety of the post-Civil War Spanish has been their broken connection to the modern. To make this connection, Gil de Biedma adopted the cultural collage from Eliot, whom he translated. In his poems little is invented: Almost everything is borrowed and recycled to make the mask through which he speaks. Most of the titles, narratives or central images hint at a foreign, classical or traditional Spanish source, or slyly refer to some bit of popular culture. A complete annotation of these sources might rival the notes to *The Wasteland* yet it would be unnecessary. Except for the occasional phrase in another language left to show through — like a tear in the new fabric that exposes some rich old upholstery underneath — the allusion in Gil de Biedma's poetry is integrated. Older sources are transformed into a new poem whose subtle layering suggests that the poet is also a fellow reader.

These allusions are stitched seamlessly together into a spare, conversational speech that Gil de Biedma uses to distance his poems from the pompous public lie. This language is made up of the dog-eared syllables that hold families, friends and lovers together: "household words worn warm with use." The inviolate Spanish home remained a refuge during the Franco era, a place where people sat down together to tell the truth. Without slipping into slang, Gil de Beidma constructs a grammatically elegant tango out of colloquial phrases. Often he writes as if he had carefully closed the shutters and turned to speak to a group of close friends, in which we are included.

In the love poems as well as in the political ones, Gil de Biedma uses this personal voice to deflate the bombast of two schools of post-Civil War poetry: *Garcilasimo* and "social poetry." In vogue just after the war, the former was a "well wrought" formalist romanticism of the most escapist, cardboard variety, supported by Franco's Ministry of Press and Propaganda to soften the regime's anti-intellectual reputation. This is why such a romantically-inclined poet as Gil de Biedma frames his lyrical passages with irony, much like Auden. Chipping away at leftist rhetoric, on the other hand, was a more delicate matter. Gil de Biedma identified himself in *Traveling Companions*, his first major volume, with the "social poets" of the anti-Franco resistance, who turned from pure lyricism toward the plight of the people. Unfortunately, "the people" celebrated in these poems were mostly rural — and this during an era marked by mass migration to the city — and the urban, educated poets took on a Soviet-inspired prophetic role, speaking for workers with whom they had little contact. In his second volume, *Morality Plays*, Gil de Biedma's poetry remains committed to social issues, not by moralistically speaking for "the people" but, more painfully, by examining his relationship to his own origins.

In his best known poem, for instance, "*Barcelona Ja No És Bona*, or My Solitary Spring Walk," he elegizes in lushly cinemagraphic images the once-elegant world of the Catalan bourgeoisie he grew up in, at the same time confessing to "a completely different attitude / I developed as an adult, / this resentment / against the class I was born into." He realizes that the immigrant workers from Southern Spain, whose exploited labor fueled the factories that supported his privileged youth, have an equal birthright to the city and will one day dominate it. Although his perspective is Marxist, he undercuts the megaphone-register public poem we might expect with the conversational, the specific and the ironic. This stripping away of coat after coat of rhetorical falseness like old paint until an authentic human voice shines through is the essence of his art.

In this and other poems, each moment is defeated, *Marienbad*-like, by the oblique reflections of another moment. And the shell-game that memory plays between these moments spirals toward a sense of loss. Like Baudelaire, Gil de Biedma is an urbanite whose idea of "nature" is a stroll among the graffitied statues of a public park. What for the romantics was a loss of nature is for him the losses inflicted by time: childhood, youth, idealism, early love or the sensuous Philippines, a somewhere-else as far away as innocence. "I have only two themes," he remarked, "myself and the passing of time."

"Myself" involves the creation of a dramatic mask rather than the naked confessionalism of much autobiographical poetry in the United States. The mythical "Jaime Gil de Biedma" invoked in the poems is not necessarily drawn directly from the poet's daily life. Like most Spanish intellectuals, Gil de Biedma earned his living apart from his literary career. The family business was the Philippine Tobacco Company, headquartered on Las Ramblas in Barcelona, for which he worked all his life, rising to the governing board as his father had before him. Except for sojourns in Manila and at Oxford, Gil de Biedma stayed rooted in his native Barcelona and did not follow many of his generation into self-exile abroad. Another private aspect of his life never treated explicitly in his poems, despite their eroticism, is his homosexuality, not only to avoid state censorship but because the gay movement did not emerge in Spain until the early 1980s. The rebellious, cosmopolitan, *maudit* mask in the poems was created, in fact, by a writer traditionally Spanish at heart: He lived near his family, entered their business, spent vacations at their ancestral country house and, like most Spaniards, considered the details of how he earned a living or whom he slept with nobody's business but his own.

When asked to compare his body of work to that of other poets of his generation, Gil de Biedma answered with characteristic economy: "It's briefer." He wrote slowly and carefully, and the selection made here includes, in much the same order, most of the poems central to his work, with the exception of a few in strict forms that do not translate well. After his collected poems appeared in 1975, he wrote little more, giving weight to the image of poetic suicide presented in *Posthumous Poems*, his final volume. In a perfect symbolic gesture, he retired both from literature and life to a town near Gerona called Ultramort, which in Catalan means "beyond death."

Gil de Biedma was a poet who outlived his era, as he himself knew best. Yet his recent cult status in Spain is only partly due to the sensationalized media accounts of his homosexuality and death from AIDS. The freedom imagined in his defiant, sensual poetry has been realized during the last decade, when Spanish cities have become an all-night whirl of bars and discos, a high-decibel celebration fed by hashish, open sexuality, *outré* fashions and the most tolerant attitudes, straight out of an Almodóvar movie. The Spanish, however, have not forgotten a generation of repression or those who helped them to transcend it. In "All Saints Day" Gil de Biedma commemorates his pilgrimage to the abandoned tomb of the Republican leader Pablo Iglesias in 1959, the year when Eisenhower's benedictory visit to Franco crushed a growing hope of overthrowing the regime. He reminds his companions from the resistance how

> that day's impression, that sun's vision
> and the head of that Spaniard laid to rest
> will live on as a symbol, as a passionate
> call to the future, in the worst of times.

Looking around Spain now, it is easy to see how far behind those "worst of times" seem to the Spanish. Yet this same Pablo Iglesias founded the Spanish Socialist Workers' Party, which has been in national power since 1982. The political rise of young anti-Franco militants has placed at the center stage of Spanish letters older resistance writers such as Gil de Biedma.

Spain is no longer a country of memories but of plans. The bridge generation of Gil de Biedma is important to understanding how the chasm created by war and dictatorship has been spanned. Gil de Biedma is not a poet of public heroics such as Whitman and Neruda, yet his private voice allowed modernity to survive in Spain during a regressive dark age. He is not a poet of revolutionary optimism but of how to remain fully alive — "if only for a moment" — under defeat. His "passionate call to the future" helped to safeguard individual freedom and the personal imagination during an era of censorship, puritanical intolerance, public poverty and police-state control. And for this reason, I suspect, he should be of particular interest to Americans, now and in "the worst of times."

James Nolan
Barcelona-San Francisco
1991

"I was born in Barcelona in 1929 and I've almost always lived here. I spent the three years of the Civil War in Nava de la Asunción, a village in the province of Segovia, where my family has a house to which I always end up returning. Going back and forth between Catalonia and Castille — or more exactly, between a middle-class life and *la vie de châteaux* — has been an important factor in forming my personal mythology. I studied Law in Barcelona and Salamanca, graduating in 1951. Since 1955 I have worked for a commercial company. My job has brought me to live for long stretches in Manila, a city I love and find a lot less exotic than Seville because I understand it better. I went bald in 1962; the loss revolted me but I wasn't obsessed by it — they say I have a nicely shaped head. I make enough money. I don't save any. I've been a leftist and probably will remain one, but for a while now I haven't been active."

O.K. Now let's assume that twelve years have gone by since I wrote the above. And going even further, let's assume the worst: our assumption — yours and mine, reader, don't forget — is absolutely true. What shall I say has happened to me in this space between paragraphs? The first, most gut-level response is: nothing. Then, after mulling it over, certain matters are unavoidable. Manila, for instance, bores me now and, on the other hand, I was fascinated by Seville, discovered for the first time in November of 1976 after having been there so many times. Also in 1974 I published my diary from 1956 — years ending in six have always been important for me — titled *Diario del artista seriamente enfermo*, and in 1980 I collected my critical essays and a few other pieces into a volume, *El pie de la letra*. Here and now I'm publishing the second edition, indetectably enlarged, of my collected poems. Finally, after all these years, I've learned, for better or worse — better and worse — how to arrange my work. A humble but absorbing apprenticeship that barely leaves time to write poems.

Maybe more could be said about this, about not writing. A lot of people ask me, I ask myself. And asking myself why I don't write inevitably spills over into another much more terrifying inquiry: why did I write? Reading, after all, is the normal thing. I have two favorite answers. First, that without realizing it, my poetry consisted in an attempt to make up an identity. Already invented and taken on, it doesn't occur to me to gamble everything as I once did in every poem I set out to write, which is what excited me. Another answer is that it was a mistake: I thought I wanted to be a poet but basically I wanted to be the poem. In a way, the worst way, I've succeeded. Like any halfway well-written poem, I'm no longer free inside, I'm all necessity and internal submission to that anguished dictator, that omniscient and ubiquitous Big Brother who never sleeps: I. Most of all I'm frightened of him, half-Caliban, half-Narcissus, listening to him grill me next to an open balcony: "What's a 50's kind of kid like you doing in a dull year like this?" *All the rest is silence.*

Jaime Gil de Biedma
1982

I

from
Compañeros de viaje (1959):

Traveling Companions

AUNQUE SEA UN INSTANTE

Aunque sea un instante, deseamos
descansar. Soñamos con dejarnos.
No sé, pero en cualquier lugar
con tal de que la vida deponga sus espinas.

Un instante, tal vez. Y nos volvemos
atrás, hacia el pasado engañoso cerrándose
sobre el mismo temor actual, que día a día
entonces también conocimos.

                   Se olvida
pronto, se olvida el sudor tantas noches,
la nerviosa ansiedad que amarga el mejor logro
llevándonos a él de antemano rendidos
sin más que ese vacío de llegar,
la indiferencia extraña de lo que ya está hecho.

Así que a cada vez que este temor,
el eterno temor que tiene nuestro rostro
nos asalta, gritamos invocando el pasado
— invocando un pasado que jamás existió —

para creer al menos que de verdad vivimos
y que la vida es más que esta pausa inmensa,
vertiginosa,
cuando la propia vocación, aquello
sobre lo cual fundamos un día nuestro ser,
el nombre que le dimos a nuestra dignidad
vemos que no era más
que un desolador deseo de esconderse.

IF ONLY FOR A MOMENT

If only for a moment, we long to stop.
We dream of taking a break from ourselves.
I'm not sure but just about anywhere
so long as life pulls in its thorns.

A moment, maybe. And we slide back
toward the two-faced past to shut out
this terror we feel, same as the one
we also knew then, day by day.

                  So many nights
how quickly we forget, forget the sweat
of upset nerves souring the greatest success,
delivering us to it half-broken from the start
except for that blank of getting it over with,
the curious indifference to what's already done.

So every time this terror ambushes us,
the terror forever wearing our face,
we cry out calling up the past —
calling up a past that never existed —

just to believe how really alive we are
and life's more than this enormous
whirling pause
when our real mission, the one
we staked our lives on then,
what we called our self-respect
was nothing more, we know,
than a mournful urge to hide.

3

IDILIO EN EL CAFÉ

Ahora me pregunto si es que toda la vida
hemos estado aquí. Pongo, ahora mismo,
la mano ante los ojos — qué latido
de la sangre en los párpados — y el vello
inmenso se confunde, silencioso,
a la mirada. Pesan las pestañas.

No sé bien de qué hablo. ¿Quiénes son,
rostros vagos nadando como en un agua pálida,
éstos aquí sentados, con nosotros vivientes?
La tarde nos empuja a ciertos bares
o entre cansados hombres en pijama.

Ven. Salgamos fuera. La noche. Queda espacio
arriba, más arriba, mucho más que las luces
que iluminan a ráfagas tus ojos agrandados.
Queda también silencio entre nosotros,
silencio
                y este beso igual que un largo túnel.

CAFÉ IDYLL

Just now I'm wondering if we've spent
our whole lives here. At once I put
my hand to my eyes — how blood
beats in my eyelids — and the gigantic
fuzz is quietly confused with what
I see. My eyelashes are growing heavy.

I'm not sure what I'm talking about. Who are
these roving faces, bobbing in milky water,
seated here next to us the living?
Evening draws us toward certain bars
or amid tired men in pajamas.

Come. Let us go then. Night. There's space
above, way above, farther than the lights
flashing brightly in your widened eyes.
There's also silence between us,
silence
                    and the long tunnel of this kiss.

ARTE POÉTICA

A Vicente Aleixandre

La nostalgia del sol en los terrados,
en el muro color paloma de cemento
— sin embargo tan vívido — y el frío
repentino que casi sobrecoge.

La dulzura, el calor de los labios a solas
en medio de la calle familiar
igual que un gran salón, donde acudieran
multitudes lejanas como seres queridos.

Y sobre todo el vértigo del tiempo,
el gran boquete abriéndose hacia dentro del alma
mientras arriba sobrenadan promesas
que desmayan, lo mismo que si espumas.

Es sin duda el momento de pensar
que el hecho de estar vivo exige algo,
acaso heroicidades — o basta, simplemente,
alguna humilde cosa común

cuya corteza de materia terrestre
tratar entre los dedos, con un poco de fe?
Palabras, por ejemplo.
Palabras de familia gastadas tibiamente.

ARS POETICA

For Vicente Aleixandre

The longing for sun on roof terraces,
on the pigeon-hued concrete wall —
yet what colors — and the abrupt
chill that almost startles.

The sweetness, warmth of lips alone
in the middle of a street cozy
as a big living room where faraway
crowds come together as loved ones.

And above all, the whirling of time's
great gap spiraling in toward the spirit
while overhead, promises float by
fizzling out like foam.

No doubt the moment's come to realize
just being alive demands something,
lofty deeds, maybe — or simply, is some
common everyday thing enough,

one whose crust of earthy stuff
fingers can fashion with a little faith?
Words, for instance.
Household words worn warm with use.

NOCHES DEL MES DE JUNIO

A Luis Cernuda

Alguna vez recuerdo
ciertas noches de junio de aquel año,
casi borrosas, de mi adolescencia
(era en mil novecientos me parece
cuarenta y nueve)
               porque en ese mes
sentía siempre una inquietud, una angustia pequeña
lo mismo que el calor que empezaba,
                        nada más
que la especial sonoridad del aire
y una disposición vagamente afectiva.

Eran las noches incurables
               y la calentura.
Las altas horas de estudiante solo
y el libro intempestivo
junto al balcón abierto de par en par (la calle
recién regada desaparecía
abajo, entre el follaje iluminado)
sin un alma que llevar a la boca.

Cuántas veces me acuerdo
de vosotras, lejanas
noches del mes de junio, cuántas veces
me saltaron las lágrimas, las lágrimas
por ser más que un hombre, cuánto quise
morir
        o soñé con venderme al diablo,
que nunca me escuchó.
                  Pero también
la vida nos sujeta porque precisamente
no es como la esperábamos.

NIGHTS IN THE MONTH OF JUNE

For Luis Cernuda

Sometimes I'm reminded
of certain June nights, almost a blur,
during that year in my teens
(it was Nineteen let me see
Forty-Nine)
                because in this month
I always felt troubled, a slight torment
just like the heat setting in,
                      nothing more
than a particular resonance in the air
and a mood of vaguely being in love.

Nights were incurable
                so was the fever.
Late-night hours of a student
alone with some unlikely book
next to balcony doors thrown open (the street,
just-washed, vanished below
among lamplit leaves)
without a soul to nourish him.

How often I think
of you, faraway nights
in the month of June, how often
I burst into tears, tears for being
more than a man, how much I wanted
to end it all
      or daydreamed of selling myself to the devil
who never took me up on it.
                  But then again
life keeps us in line exactly because
it never turns out as we hoped.

9

INFANCIA Y CONFESIONES

A Juan Goytisolo

Cuando yo era más joven
(bueno, en realidad, será mejor decir
muy joven)
        algunos años antes
de conoceros y
recién llegado a la ciudad,
a menudo pensaba en la vida.
                Mi familia
era bastante rica y yo estudiante.

Mi infancia eran recuerdos de una casa
con escuela y despensa y llave en el ropero,
de cuando las familias
acomodadas,
           como su nombre indica,
veraneaban infinitamente
en *Villa Estefanía* o en *La Torre
del Mirador*
          y más allá continuaba el mundo
con senderos de grava y cenadores
rústicos, decorado de hortensias pomposas,
todo ligeramente egoísta y caduco.
Yo nací (perdonadme)
en la edad de la pérgola y el tenis.

La vida, sin embargo, tenía extraños límites
y lo que es más extraño: una cierta tendencia
retráctil.
       Se contaban historias penosas,
inexplicables sucedidos
dónde no se sabía, caras tristes,
sótanos fríos como templos.
              Algo sordo
perduraba a lo lejos
y era posible, lo decían en casa,
quedarse ciego de un escalofrío.

De mi pequeño reino afortunado
me quedó esta costumbre de calor
y una imposible propensión al mito.

CHILDHOOD AND CONFESSIONS

For Juan Goytisolo

When I was younger
(okay, actually better to say
really young)
         a few years before
getting to know all of you and
just arrived in the city,
I thought a lot about life.
              My family
was pretty rich and I, a student.

My childhood was memories of a house
with school and pantry and key in the closet
from those days when well-to-do
families,
         as the term implies,
summered indefinitely
at "Villa Stephany" or "Broadview
Belvedere"
         and the world outside
led to gravel footpaths and countrified
galleries decked out with pompous hydrangeas,
everything just a touch selfish and senile.
I was born (forgive me)
in the era of gazebos and lawn tennis.

Life, at the same time, had weird limitations
and even weirder: a certain inclination
to pull inward.
           Upsetting stories were told,
puzzling goings on,
where was never clear, sad faces,
basements cold as temples.
           A deafness
was entrenched in the distance
and as they said at home, you could
go blind from catching a chill.

From my privileged little kingdom
I've held onto this habit of warmth
and an impossible propensity for myth.

LAS GRANDES ESPERANZAS

Le mort saisit le vif

Las grandes esperanzas están todas
puestas sobre vosotros,
                          así dicen
los señores solemnes, y también:
                          Tomad.
Aquí la escuela y la despensa, sois mayores,
libres de disponer
                    sin imprudentes
romanticismos, por supuesto.
La verdad, que debierais estar agradecidos.
Pero ya veis, nos bastan las grandes esperanzas
y todas están puestas en vosotros.

Cada mañana vengo,
cada mañana vengo para ver
lo que ayer no existía
cómo en el Nombre del Padre se ha dispuesto,
y cómo cada fecha libre fue entregada,
dada en aval, suscrita por
los padres nuestros
                    de cada día.

Cada mañana vengo para ver
que todo está servido (me saludan,
al entrar, levantando un momento los ojos)
y cada mañana me pregunto,
cada mañana me pregunto cuántos somos
nosotros, y de quién venimos,
y qué precio pagamos por esa confianza.

O quizá
no venimos tampoco para eso.
La cuestión se reduce a estar vivo un instante,
aunque sea un instante no más,
                          a estar vivo
justo en ese minuto
cuando nos escapamos
al mejor de los mundos imposibles.
En donde nada importa,
nada absolutamente — ni siquiera
las grandes esperanzas que están puestas
todas sobre nosotros, todas,
                          y así pesan.

GREAT EXPECTATIONS

Le mort saisit le vif

"All of our great expectations
are placed upon each of you,"
                              or so say
the solemn gentlemen, and then:
                              "Here,
take the school and pantry, you're adults,
free to run things
                  without any romantic
shenanigans, of course.
Truth is you should all be thankful.
But you see, the great expectations
placed upon you are enough for us."

Every morning I show up,
every morning I show up to observe
how what didn't exist yesterday
has been ordained in the Name of the Father,
how every free day's paid to the account,
secured as collateral, underwritten by
the daily bread
                of our fathers.

Every morning I show up to observe
how everything has its place (walking in,
they greet me, raising their eyes a moment),
every morning I ask myself,
every morning I wonder how many we are
and who sent us here
and what price we pay for this trust.

Or perhaps
we didn't come here for this either.
It all boils down to being alive for a moment,
if only for a moment, no more,
                              being alive
at the exact minute
when we break away into
the best of all impossible worlds.
Where not a thing matters,
absolutely nothing — not even
the great expectations laid
upon us, all hanging
                    so heavy.

DE AHORA EN ADELANTE

Como después de un sueño,
no acertaría
a decir en qué instante sucedió.
                              Llamaban.
Algo, ya comenzado, no admitía espera.

Me sentí extraño al principio,
lo reconozco — tantos años
que pasaron igual que si en la luna . . .
Decir exactamente qué buscaba,
mi esperanza cuál fue, no me es posible
decirlo ahora,
                    porque en un instante
determinado todo vaciló: llamaban.
Y me sentí cercano.
Un poco de aire libre,
algo tan natural como un rumor
crece si se le escucha de repente.

Pero ya desde ahora siempre será lo mismo.
Porque de pronto el tiempo se ha colmado
y no da para más. Cada mañana
trae, como dice Auden, verbos irregulares
que es preciso aprender, o decisiones
penosas y que aguardan examen.
                                  Todavía
hay quien cuenta conmigo. Amigos míos,
o mejor: compañeros, necesitan,
quieren lo mismo que yo quiero
y me quieren a mí también, igual
que yo me quiero.

Así que apenas puedo recordar
qué fue de varios años de mi vida,
o adónde iba cuando desperté
y no me encontré solo.

FROM NOW ON

As after a dream,
I couldn't pinpoint
the moment it happened.
                              They called.
Once started, something wouldn't wait.

At first I felt odd,
I confess — so many years
had slipped by as if on the moon . . . .
Right now I can't describe
exactly what I was looking for
or what my expectations were
                              because in one
fell swoop everything wavered: they called.
And I felt close.
A little fresh air,
something normal as whispering
swells if you suddenly listen to it.

But it'll always be that way from now on.
Because suddenly time has brimmed over,
has nothing more to offer. Every morning,
as Auden says, delivers its irregular verbs
to be memorized or distressing decisions
that await further study.
                              Still
there are those who count on me. My friends,
or better put, my companions need
and love what I love
and they also love me,
just as I love myself.

This is why I can barely recall
what happened to several years of my life
or where I was heading when I woke up
and found I wasn't alone.

LOS APARECIDOS

Fue esta mañana misma,
en mitad de la calle.

       Yo esperaba
con los demás, al borde de la señal de cruce,
y de pronto he sentido como un roce ligero,
como casi una súplica en la manga.

             Luego,
mientras precipitadamente atravesaba,
la visión de unos ojos terribles, exhalados
yo no sé desde qué vacío doloroso.

Ocurre que esto sucede
demasiado a menudo.

          Y sin embargo,
al menos en algunos de nosotros,
queda una estela de malestar furtivo,
un cierto sentimiento de culpabilidad.

           Recuerdo
también, en una hermosa tarde
que regresaba a casa . . . Una mujer
se desplomó a mi lado replegándose
sobre sí misma, silenciosamente
y con una increíble lentitud — la tuve
por las axilas, un momento el rostro,
viejo, casi pegado al mío.
Luego, sin comprender aún,
incorporó unos ojos donde nada
se leía, sino la pura privación
que me daba las gracias.

         Me volví
penosamente a verla calle abajo.

No sé cómo explicarlo, es
lo mismo que si todo,
lo mismo que si el mundo alrededor
estuviese parado
pero continuase en movimiento
cínicamente, como
si nada, como si nada fuese verdad.
Cada aparición
que pasa, cada cuerpo en pena
no anuncia muerte, dice que la muerte estaba
ya entre nosotros sin saberlo.

HOMELESS GHOSTS

It happened just this morning
in the middle of the street.

                       I was waiting
with others at the edge of a crosswalk
when suddenly I felt a slight pulling,
almost a plea tugged at my sleeve.
                            Then
while I was crossing quickly
the sight of two horrifying eyes shot out
from I don't know what aching blankness.

This sort of incident takes place
far too often.
                But yet,
at least in some of us,
it leaves a trace of private uneasiness,
a certain sense of guilt.
                  I also
remember one gorgeous afternoon
on the way home . . . a woman
collapsed next to me, silently
doubling over in unbelievably
slow-motion — I held onto her
by the armpits, her old face almost
plastered next to mine for a moment.
Then, just as bewildering,
a pair of eyes took shape
in which nothing could be read
but an utter need thanking me.
                      I turned
to painfully watch her walk down the street.

I can't explain it,
it's as if everything,
like the world around you
came screeching to a halt
yet cynically kept
spinning, as if nothing,
nothing were true.
Every homeless ghost
who walks by, each body in agony
isn't heralding death but saying,
little do we know it, death's already among us.

              Vienen
de allá, del otro lado del fondo sulfuroso,
de las sordas
minas del hambre y de la multitud.
Y ni siquiera saben quiénes son:
desenterrados vivos.

They come
from over there, from the other shore
of the sulphurous depths, from deaf
minepits of hunger and the masses.
And even they don't know who they are:
the unburied living.

PIAZZA DEL POPOLO

(Habla María Zambrano)

Fue una noche como ésta.
Estaba el balcón abierto
igual que hoy está, de par
en par. Me llegaba el denso
olor del río cercano
en la oscuridad. Silencio.
Silencio de multitud,
impresionante silencio
alrededor de una voz
que hablaba: presentimiento
religioso era el futuro.
Aquí en la Plaza del Pueblo
se oía latir — y yo,
junto a ese balcón abierto,
era también un latido
escuchando. Del silencio,
por encima de la plaza,
creció de repente un trueno
de voces juntas. Cantaban.
Y yo cantaba con ellos.
Oh sí, cantábamos todos
otra vez, qué movimiento,
qué revolución de soles
en el alma! Sonrieron
rostros de muertos amigos
saludándome a lo lejos
borrosos — pero qué jóvenes,
qué jóvenes sois los muertos! —
y una entera muchedumbre
me prorrumpió desde dentro
toda en pie. Bajo la luz
de un cielo puro y colérico
era la misma canción
en las plazas de otro pueblo,
era la misma esperanza,
el mismo latido inmenso
de un solo ensordecedor
corazón a voz en cuello.
Sí, reconozco esas voces
cómo cantaban. Me acuerdo.
Aquí en el fondo del alma
absorto, sobre lo trémulo
de la memoria desnuda,

PIAZZA DEL POPOLO

(María Zambrano speaks)

It was a night like tonight,
the balcony doors wide
open just as they are
now. I caught the heavy
scent of the nearby river
in the darkness. Silence.
The crowd's silence,
an unfathomable silence
enveloping one voice
speaking: the future,
a religious premonition.
Here in People's Plaza
you heard it throbbing —
I, by this open balcony,
was also a listening
throb. From the silence
a thunderclap of voices
in unison suddenly rose
over the plaza. They sang.
And I sang with them.
Oh yes, we sang together
again, what a commotion,
what an upheaval of suns
in the spirit. Dead friends'
faces, hazy in the distance,
greeted me smiling — how young,
how young you dead stay! —
and inside me a whole crowd
burst out singing, jumping
to their feet. In the light
of a clear, hot-tempered sky
there was this same song
in the plazas of another people,
there was this same hope,
the same enormous throbbing
of a single deafening heart
swelling to a loud shout.
Yes, I recognize those voices,
how they sang. I remember.
Here at my spirit's astonished
core, in the shaking of naked
memory, everything is happening

todo se está repitiendo.
Y vienen luego las noches
interminables, el éxodo
por la derrota adelante,
hostigados, bajo el cielo
que ansiosamente los ojos
interrogan. Y de nuevo
alguien herido, que ya
le conozco en el acento,
alguien herido pregunta,
alguien herido pregunta
en la oscuridad. Silencio.
A cada instante que irrumpe
palpitante, como un eco
más interior, otro instante
responde agónico.
    Cierro
los ojos, pero los ojos
del alma siguen abiertos
hasta el dolor. Y me tapo
los oídos y no puedo
dejar de oír estas voces
que me cantan aquí dentro.

all over again. And then
come the nights without end,
the exodus from defeat ahead,
the tortured, their eyes
anxiously questioning the sky.
Again somebody wounded — I know
him already by his accent —
somebody wounded asks,
somebody wounded asks
in the darkness. Silence.
To every moment that charges in
zinging, another moment answers
in agony, a deeper echo.

        I shut
my eyes but the spirit's eyes
stay open till it hurts. And I
cover my ears but can't stop
hearing these voices
singing to me — here inside.

II

from
Moralidades (1966):

Morality Plays

Finally to my friends,
traveling companions,
and especially among them
to you, Carlos, Ángel,
Alfonso and Pepe, Gabriel
and Gabriel, Pepe (Caballero)
and to my nephew Miguel,
Joseagustín and Blas de Otero,

to you sinners
like me, ashamed as I am
of the beatings I've been spared,
rich kids by birth,
writers of social poetry
out of a bad conscience,
I also make a special dedication.

from "In the Name of Today"

BARCELONA JA NO ÉS BONA, o
MI PASEO SOLITARIO EN PRIMAVERA

A Fabián Estapé

> *Este despedazado anfiteatro,*
> *ímpio honor de los dioses, cuya afrenta*
> *publica el amarillo jaramago,*
> *ya reducido a trágico teatro,*
> *¡oh fábula del tiempo! representa*
> *cuánta fue su grandeza y es su estrago.*

– Rodrigo Caro

En los meses de aquella primavera
pasaron por aquí seguramente
más de una vez.
Entonces, los dos eran muy jóvenes
y tenían el Chrysler amarillo y negro.
Los imagino al mediodía, por la avenida de los tilos,
la capota del coche salpicada de sol,
o quizá en Miramar, llegando a los jardines,
mientras que sobre el fondo del puerto y la ciudad
se mecen las sombrillas del restaurante al aire libre,
y las conversaciones, y la música,
fundiéndose al rumor de los neumáticos
sobre la grava del paseo.
                              Sólo por un instante
se destacan los dos a pleno sol
con los trajes que he visto en las fotografías:
él examina un coche muchísimo mas caro
— un Duesemberg *sport* con doble parabrisas,
bello como una máquina de guerra —
y ella se vuelve a mí, quizá esperándome,
y el vaivén de las rosas de la pérgola
parpadea en la sombra
de sus pacientes ojos de embarazada.
Era en el año de la Exposición.

Así yo estuve aquí
dentro del vientre de mi madre,
y es verdad que algo oscuro, que algo anterior me trae
por estos sitios destartalados.
Más aún que los árboles y la naturaleza
o que el susurro del agua corriente
furtiva, reflejándose en las hojas
— y eso que ya a mis años
se empieza a agradecer la primavera — ,

BARCELONA JA NO ÉS BONA, or
MY SOLITARY SPRING WALK

For Fabian Estapé

This amphitheater, shattered by age,
honor of the gods profaned, whose shame
the yellow mustard plant proclaims,
reduced to this last tragic stage.
O legend of time! that now portrays
the sweep of its grandeur and decay.

– Rodrigo Caro

They passed by here
probably more than once
in those spring months.
They were both really young then
and had a two-toned Chrysler, yellow and black.
I picture them at noon on the linden-lined avenue,
carhood dappled with sunlight
or just arriving, maybe, at the Miramar's gardens
while parasols of the open-air restaurant,
conversation and music swirled
above the backdrop of port and city,
melting into the murmur of tires
rolling over driveway gravel.
                Only for a moment
they step forward into bright sunlight
in clothes I've seen in old photos:
he inspects a much more expensive car —
a Duesemberg sports coupe with dual windshields,
as impressive as a tank —
and she turns toward me, expectantly perhaps,
while the shimmer of trellised roses
flutters in the shade
of her patient, pregnant eyes.
This was in the year of the International Exhibition.

This way I was present, too,
inside my mother's womb
and it's true some darkness, some beforeness
lures me back to these places gone to seed.
Even more than trees and nature
or the gurgle of hidden trickles
of water mirrored in flickering leaves —
and believe me, at my age now
you learn to be grateful for spring —

yo busco en mis paseos los tristes edificios,
las estatuas manchadas con lápiz de labios,
los rincones del parque pasados de moda
en donde, por la noche, se hacen el amor . . .
Y a la nostalgia de una edad feliz
y de dinero fácil, tal como la contaban,
se mezcla un sentimiento bien distinto
que aprendí de mayor,
                              este resentimiento
contra la clase en que nací,
y que se complace también al ver mordida,
ensuciada la feria de sus vanidades
por el tiempo y las manos del resto de los hombres.

Oh mundo de mi infancia, cuya mitología
se asocia — bien lo veo —
con el capitalismo de empresa familiar!
Era ya un poco tarde
incluso en Cataluña, pero la *pax* burguesa
reinaba en los hogares y en las fábricas,
sobre todo en las fábricas — Rusia estaba muy lejos
y muy lejos Detroit.
Algo de aquel momento queda en estos palacios
y en estas perspectivas desiertas bajo el sol,
cuyo destino ya nadie recuerda.
Todo fue una ilusión, envejecida
como la maquinaria de sus fábricas,
o como la casa en Sitges, o en Caldetas,
heredada también por el hijo mayor.

Sólo montaña arriba, cerca ya del castillo,
de sus fosos quemados por los fusilamientos,
dan señales de vida los murcianos.
Y yo subo despacio por las escalinatas
sintiéndome observado, tropezando en las piedras
en donde las higueras agarran sus raíces,
mientras oigo a estos chavas nacidos en el Sur
hablarse en catalán, y pienso, a un mismo tiempo,
en mi pasado y en su porvenir.

Sean ellos sin más preparación
que su instinto de vida
más fuertes al final que el patrón que les paga
y que el *salta-taulells* que les desprecia:
que la ciudad les pertenezca un día.
Como les pertenece esta montaña,
este despedazado anfiteatro
de las nostalgias de una burguesía.

what I seek out in my strolls are sad buildings,
statues lipsticked with graffiti,
the now unpopular park corners
where at night people come to make love . . . .
And the nostalgia for a golden age
of easy money, as they told it,
blends with a completely different attitude
I developed as an adult,
                              this resentment
against the class I was born into,
so that it's equally gratifying to see
their vanity fair shopworn and smudged
by time and the hands of everyone else.

O world of my childhood, whose myths
are connected — I so plainly see —
to the capitalism of the family business!
Even then it was a bit late,
even in Catalonia, but the *pax* bourgeois
ruled in homes and factories,
particularly in factories — Russia was a million
miles away and so was Detroit.
Something of that moment clings to these mansions,
to these emptied vistas of sunlight
whose fate everyone's forgotten.
It was all a facade, grown creaky
as its factory machinery
or its summer houses in Sitges or Caldetas,
also passed down to the eldest son.

Only up on the mountain, near the castle
with its moats blackened by firing squads,
do the Southern immigrants show any life.
As I slowly mount the flight of steps,
feeling watched, stumbling against stones
where fig trees hang on by their roots,
while I hear these hicks born in the South
rattling on in Catalan, I consider my past
and at the same time, their future.

Let this city be theirs one day,
with no better preparation
than their survival instincts, stronger
in the end than the bosses who pay them
and the Catalan clerks who look down on them.
As this mountain is theirs already,
this amphitheater shattered into bits
of nostalgia for a lost ruling class.

NOCHE TRISTE DE OCTUBRE, 1959

A Juan Marsé

Definitivamente
parece confirmarse que este invierno
que viene, será duro.

Adelantaron
las lluvias, y el Gobierno,
reunido en consejo de ministros,
no se sabe si estudia a estas horas
el subsidio de paro
o el derecho al despido,
o si sencillamente, aislado en un océano,
se limita a esperar que la tormenta pase
y llegue el día, el día en que, por fin,
las cosas dejen de venir mal dadas.

En la noche de octubre,
mientras leo entre líneas el periódico,
me he parado a escuchar el latido
del silencio en mi cuarto, las conversaciones
de los vecinos acostándose,

                todos esos rumores
que recobran de pronto una vida
y un significado propio, misterioso.

Y he pensado en los miles de seres humanos,
hombres y mujeres que en este mismo instante,
con el primer escalofrío.
han vuelto a preguntarse por sus preocupaciones,
por su fatiga anticipada,
por su ansiedad para este invierno,

mientras que afuera llueve.
Por todo el litoral de Cataluña llueve
con verdadera crueldad, con humo y nubes bajas,
ennegreciendo muros,
goteando fábricas, filtrándose
en los talleres mal iluminados.
Y el agua arrastra hacia la mar semillas
incipientes, mezcladas en el barro,
árboles, zapatos cojos, utensilios
abandonados y revuelto todo
con las primeras Letras protestadas.

SAD OCTOBER NIGHT, 1959

For Juan Marsé

Something definitely tells me
this coming winter
is going to be a hard one.

The rains
came early and it's anyone's guess
if the government in its cabinet session
is considering unemployment compensation
or the right to unemploy
or if plainly cut off out at sea,
it just has to wait out the storm
and for the day to dawn, that day
when the bad luck finally runs out.

On this October night,
as I read between the lines of the newspaper,
I've paused to listen to the heartbeat
of silence in my room, to conversations
of neighbors going to bed,
                            all these whispers
that suddenly take on a separate life
with a mysterious meaning all its own.

And I've thought of thousands of humans,
men and women who at this very moment,
with the first shiver, have slipped back
into worrying about their problems,
about the daily grind they foresee,
about their fear of this winter,

while outside it's raining.
Along the whole Catalonian coast it rains
with real cruelty, with smoke and low clouds,
blackening walls,
dripping into factories, seeping
into poorly-lit workshops.
And gullies of water drag down to the sea
sprouting seeds mixed in with the muck,
trees, single shoes, tossed out
tools, everything churning together,
the first protests with the missed payments.

PARÍS, POSTAL DEL CIELO

Ahora, voy a contaros
cómo también yo estuve en París, y fui dichoso.

Era en los buenos años de mi juventud,
los años de abundancia
del corazón, cuando dejar atrás padres y patria
es sentirse más libre para siempre, y fue
en verano, aquel verano
de la huelga y las primeras canciones de Brassens,
y de la hermosa historia
de casi amor.

Aún vive en mi memoria aquella noche,
recién llegado. Todavía contemplo,
bajo el Pont Saint Michel, de la mano, en silencio,
la gran luna de agosto suspensa entre las torres
de Notre Dame, y azul
de un imposible el río tantas veces soñado
— *It's too romantic*, como tú me dijiste
al retirar los labios.

¿En qué sitio perdido
de tu país, en qué rincón de Norteamérica
y en el cuarto de quién, a las horas más feas,
cuando sueñes morir no te importa en qué brazos,
te llegará, lo mismo
que ahora a mí me llega, ese calor de gentes
y la luz de aquel cielo rumoroso
tranquilo, sobre el Sena?

Como sueño vivido hace ya mucho tiempo,
como aquella canción
de entonces, así vuelve al corazón,
en un instante, en una intensidad, la historia
de nuestro amor,
confundiendo los días y sus noches,
los momentos felices,
los reproches

y aquel viaje — camino de la cama —
en un vagón del Metro Étoile-Nation.

PARIS, POSTCARD FROM HEAVEN

Now let me tell all of you about
when I was in Paris, too. And how happy I was.

It was in the heyday of my youth
when my heart was brimming over
and just leaving kin and country
felt like being set free, forever.
And it was summer, that summer
of the strike and Brassens' first songs
and of a beautiful
love story — almost.

I remember that night when I'd just arrived
as if it were yesterday. Standing silently
hand-in-hand under the Pont Saint Michel,
I can still see that enormous August moon
slung between the spires of Notre Dame,
the river an unnatural blue, dreamed of so often —
"It's too romantic," as you informed me,
turning your lips away.

Where will you be, in what godforsaken hole
of your country, in which pocket of the U.S.A.,
in whose room, at the grimmest moments
when wanting to die in anyone's arms
it comes back to you, just
as I'm seeing it now, that feverish crowd
and the glow of that murmuring
motionless sky over the Seine?

Like a fantasy lived out years ago,
like the song they were playing
then, the heart rushes backward like this
in an immediacy, in an intensity: our love,
this story,
mixing up days and nights,
wonderful times,
accusations

and that ride — all the way to bed —
on the metro line Étoile-Nation.

DE AQUÍ A LA ETERNIDAD

Ya soy dichoso, ya soy feliz
porque triunfante llegué a Madrid,
llegué a Madrid.

– "La viejecita," Coro

Lo primero, sin duda, es este ensanchamiento
de la respiración, casi angustioso.
Y la especial sonoridad del aire,
como una gran campana en el vacío,
acercándome olores
de jara de la sierra,
más perfumados por la lejanía,
y de tantos veranos juntos
de mi niñez.

        Luego está la glorieta
preliminar, con su pequeño intento de jardín,
mundo abreviado, renovado y puro
sin demasiada convicción, y al fondo
la previsible estatua y el pórtico de acceso
a la magnífica avenida,
a la famosa capital.

Y la vida, que adquiere
carácter panorámico,
inmensidad de instante también casi angustioso
— como de amanecer en campamento
o portal de belén — , la vida va espaciándose
otra vez bajo el cielo enrarecido
mientras que aceleramos.

Porque hay siempre algo más, algo espectral
como invisiblemente sustraído,
y sin embargo verdadero.
Yo pienso en zonas lívidas, en calles
o en caminos perdidos hacia pueblos
a lo lejos, igual que en un belén,
y vuelvo a ver esquinas de ladrillo injuriado
y pasos a nivel solitarios, y miradas
asomándose a vernos, figuras diminutas
que se quedan atrás para siempre, en la memoria,
como peones camineros.

Y esto es todo, quizás. Alrededor
se ciernen las fachadas, y hay gentes en la acera
frente al primer semáforo.

FROM HERE TO ETERNITY

Now I'm in luck, now I'm happy
because I made the big time to Madrid,
I made it to Madrid.

– Chorus, "The Little Old Lady"

Absolutely the first sign is this dilated
breathing, almost agonizing.
And a certain vibrato in the air
like a huge bell tolling through emptiness,
bringing closer the scent
of mountain rockrose
sweetened by distance,
and of so many of my childhood
summers all at once.

Then there's the outlying
traffic circle with its modest effort at a garden,
"a minaturized world, renewed and fresh" —
none too convincing — and in the background
the inevitable statue and the portico
opening onto the magnificent avenue
into the famous capital.

And life, taking on
a panoramic quality,
an instant immensity again almost agonizing —
like a campsite at dawn or the archway
to a nativity scene — life keeps unfurling
anew under a narrowing sky
as we speed by.

Because there's always something else,
ghostly, imperceptibly missing
and yet so there.
I ponder bluish-grey zones, streets
or roads disappearing toward towns
in the distance as in a Christmas diorama,
and I glance back at beat-up brick corners
and lonely grade-crossings, at stares
peering out to take us in, tiny figures
left behind in memory forever
like men working on the road.

Maybe that's all there ever was. On both sides
storefronts blossom and the sidewalk's full
of people in front of the first stoplight.

Cuando el rojo se apague torceremos
a la derecha,
hacia los barrios bien establecidos
de una vez para todas, con marquesas
y cajistas honrados de insigne tradición.
Ya estamos en Madrid, como quien dice.

When the red light changes we swerve
to the right
toward neighborhoods established long ago,
once and for all, with marquises and printers
revered in their illustrious tradition.
Here we are in Madrid, as anyone can see.

MAÑANA DE AYER, DE HOY

Es la lluvia sobre el mar.
  En la abierta ventana,
contemplándola, descansas
  la sién en el cristal.

Imagen de unos segundos,
  quieto en el contraluz,
tu cuerpo distinto, aún
  de la noche desnudo.

Y te vuelves hacia mí,
  sonriéndome. Yo pienso
en cómo ha pasado el tiempo,
  y te recuerdo así.

YESTERDAY MORNING, TODAY

You rest your temple against
    the open window pane
watching rain falling down
    over the ocean.

In a split-second image —
    your body outlined
serenely in half-light, still
    naked from the night.

And then you turn toward me,
    smiling. I'm thinking
so much has changed but this
    is how I remember you.

DÍAS DE PAGSANJÁN

Como los sueños, más allá
    de la idea del tiempo,
hechos sueños de sueño os llevo,
    días de Pagsanján.

En el calor, tras la espesura,
    vuelve el río a latir
moteado, como un reptil.
    Y en la atmósfera oscura

bajo los árboles en flor,
    — relucientes, mojados,
cuando a la noche nos bañábamos —
    los cuerpos de los dos.

DAYS IN PAGSANJAN

Dreams like these beyond
    the scope of time —
I conjure days turned to dreams
    from sleep in Pagsanjan.

Speckled as a reptile,
    the river bends to beat
under trees in flower
    through the jungle heat.

And in the darkened air —
    when we swam at night,
glistening and wet —
    both our bodies there.

LOCA

La noche, que es siempre ambigua,
  te enfurece — color
de ginebra mala, son
  tus ojos unas bichas.

Yo sé que vas a romper
  en insultos y en lágrimas
histéricas. En la cama,
  luego, te calmaré

con besos que me da pena
  dártelos. Y al dormir
te apretarás contra mí
  como una perra enferma.

QUEEN

Always ambiguous, the night
   makes you rage — pits
of vipers, your eyes turn
   the color of cheap gin.

I'm sure you'll shatter
   into insults, hysterical
crying and later in bed
   I'll soothe you

with kisses it grieves me
   to give. Dozing off
you'll snuggle next to me
   like a sick bitch.

LA NOVELA DE UN JOVEN POBRE

Se llamaba Pacífico,
Pacífico Ricaport,
de Santa Rita en Pampanga,
en el centro de Luzón,

y todavía le quedaba
un ligero acento pampangueño
cuando se impacientaba
y en los momentos tiernos,

precisamente al recordar,
compadecido de sí mismo,
desde sus años de capital
su infancia de campesino,

en las noches laborables
— más acá del bien y el mal —
de las barras de los bares
de la calle de Isaac Peral,

porque era pobre y muy sensible,
y guapo además, que es peor,
sobre todo en los países
sin industrialización,

y eran vagos sus medios de vida
lo mismo que sus historias,
que sus dichas y desdichas
y sus llamadas telefónicas.

Cuántas noches suspirando
en el local ya vacío,
vino a sentarse a mi lado
y le ofrecí un cigarrillo.

En esas horas miserables
en que nos hacen compañía
hasta las manchas de nuestro traje,
hablábamos de la vida

y el pobre se lamentaba
de lo que hacían con él:
"Me han echado a patadas
de tantos cuartos de hotel . . . "

Adónde habrás ido a parar,
Pacífico, viejo amigo,
tres años mas viejo ya?
Debes tener veinticinco.

TALE OF A POOR YOUNG MAN

His name was Pacífico,
Pacífico Ricaport,
from Santa Rita in Pampanga,
the heart of Luzon,

and he still had a trace
of the Pampangan accent
whenever he lost patience
or in tender moments

feeling sorry for himself,
exactly when he remembered
growing up in the country
after his years in Manila

spending weekday nights
this side of good and evil
at the bars of the joints
on Isaac Peral Street

because poor, really sensitive,
he was good-looking, too,
which is worse, particularly
in an underdeveloped country,

and his livelihood, a bit vague,
along with his stories,
his good and bad luck
and his telephone calls.

So many nights, sighing
to himself in the emptied bar,
he'd saunter over to sit by me
and I'd offer him a cigarette.

In those forlorn hours,
when even stained clothes
could keep us entertained,
we'd talk about life

and the poor guy would complain
about what they'd done to him:
"I've been booted out
of so many hotel rooms . . . . "

Pacífico, old buddy,
three years older now,
where have you ended up?
You must be twenty-five.

CANCIÓN DE ANIVERSARIO

Porque son ya seis años desde entonces,
porque no hay en la tierra, todavía,
nada que sea tan dulce como una habitación
para dos, si es tuya y mía;
porque hasta el tiempo, ese pariente pobre
que conoció mejores días,
parece hoy partidario de la felicidad,
cantemos, alegría!

Y luego levantémonos más tarde,
como domingo. Que la mañana plena
se nos vaya en hacer otra vez el amor,
pero mejor: de otra manera
que la noche no puede imaginarse,
mientras el cuarto se nos puebla
de sol y vecindad tranquila, igual que el tiempo,
y de historia serena.

El eco de los días de placer,
el deseo, la música acordada
dentro en el corazón, y que yo he puesto apenas
en mis poemas, por romántica;
todo el perfume, todo el pasado infiel,
lo que fue dulce y da nostalgia,
¿no ves cómo se sume en la realidad que entonces
soñabas y soñaba?

La realidad — no demasiado hermosa —
con sus inconvenientes de ser dos,
sus vergonzosas noches de amor sin deseo
y de deseo sin amor,
que ni en seis siglos de dormir a solas
las pagaríamos. Y con
sus transiciones vagas, de la traición al tedio,
del tedio a la traición.

La vida no es un sueño, tú ya sabes
que tenemos tendencia a olvidarlo.
Pero un poco de sueño, no más, un si es no es
por esta vez, callándonos
el resto de la historia, y un instante
— mientras que tú y yo nos deseamos
feliz y larga vida en común — , estoy seguro
que no puede hacer daño.

ANNIVERSARY SONG

Because six years have gone by since then,
because there's still nothing on earth,
nothing so sweet as a room
for two, if it's yours and mine;
because even time, that poor relation
who has seen better days,
is waving a flag for happiness today:
let's sing for joy!

And then let's get up late
like on Sunday. Let's linger
the whole morning long making love
again but better: in another way
night can't even imagine
while our room, just like time,
fills with sunlight, quiet intimacy
and the serenity of the ages.

Echo of our pleasure days,
desire, music remembered
inside the heart, so romantic
I've barely put it in my poems;
all the fragrance, unfaithful past,
what was sweet and inspires longing,
don't you see how everything you and I
once dreamed is overwhelmed by what is?

Reality — not a pretty sight —
with its awkward details of being two,
shameful nights of love without desire
and desire without love
we couldn't atone for in six centuries
of sleeping alone. And its enigmatic
shifts from betrayal to boredom,
boredom back to betrayal.

No, life's not a dream, and you know
we both tend to forget it.
But a little dreaming, that's all,
a smidgen for this occasion, hushing up
about the rest of the story, and a moment
when you and I wish each other
a long and happy life together —
I doubt it can do any harm.

EN EL CASTILLO DE LUNA

En el castillo de Luna
Tenéis al anciano preso.

     .   .   .

Cansadas ya las paredes
de guardar tan largo tiempo
a quien recibieron mozo
y ya le ven cano y ciego.

   – Romancero de
      Bernando del Carpio

Me digo que yo tenía
sólo diez años entonces,
que tú eras un hombre joven
y empezabas a vivir.
Y pienso en todo este tiempo,
que ha sido mi vida entera,
y en el poco que te queda
para intentar ser feliz.

Hoy te miran cano y viejo,
ya con la muerte en el alma,
las paredes de la casa
donde esperó tu mujer
tantas noches, tantos años,
y vuelves hecho un destrozo,
llenos de sombra los ojos
que casi no pueden ver.

En abril del treinta y nueve,
cuando entraste, primavera
embellecía la escena
de nuestra guerra civil.
Y era azul el cielo, claras
las aguas, y se pudrían
en las zanjas removidas
los muertos de mil en mil.

Ésta es la misma hermosura
que entonces abandonabas:
bajo las frescas acacias
desfila la juventud,
a cuerpo — chicos y chicas —
con los libros bajo el brazo.
Qué patético fracaso
la belleza y la salud.

IN LUNA CASTLE

In Luna Castle they hold
the old man prisoner.

　　　．　．　．

The walls are growing tired
of guarding all this time
one they welcomed as a youth
and now find gray and blind.

– The Romancer
of Bernardo del Carpio

Then I was only ten,
I tell myself, when
you were a young man
just beginning to live.
I think about all this time
that's been my whole life,
and the scrap left for you
to try for a little happiness.

Today the walls of the house
where your wife kept watch
so many nights, so many years,
witness you arrive old and gray,
death already in your bones.
You come home a living wreck,
eyes so crowded with shadows
they can barely see.

In April of Thirty-Nine,
when you went in,
spring was redecorating
our civil war landscape.
The sky was so blue, waters
so clear — and the dead rotted
thousands upon thousands
in freshly dug ditches.

This is the same scenery
you walked away from then:
under blooming mimosas
the youth, boys and girls,
march by in double-file
with books under their arms.
What a pathetic waste
of health and good looks.

Y los años en la cárcel,
como un tajo dividiendo
aquellos y estos momentos
de buen sol primaveral,
son un boquete en el alma
que no puedes tapar nunca,
una mina de amargura
y espantosa irrealidad.

Siete mil trescientos días
uno por uno vividos
con sus noches, confundidos
en una sola visión,
donde se juntan el hambre
y el mal olor de las mantas
y el frío en las madrugadas
y el frío en el corazón.

Ahora vuelve a la vida
y a ser libre, si es que puedes;
aunque es tarde y no te queden
esperanzas por cumplir,
siempre se obstina en ser dulce,
en merecer ser vivida
de alguna manera mínima
la vida en nuestro país.

Serás uno más, perdido,
viviendo de algún trabajo
deprimente y mal pagado,
soñando en algo mejor
que no llega. Quizá entonces
comprendas que no estás solo,
que nuestra España de todos
se parece a una prisión.

Some poets of the 50's Generation: José Agustín Goytisolo, Jaime Gil de Biedma, Carlos Barral, Yvonne Barral, Gabriel Celaya, and Amparo Gastón. Barcelona, 1962

UN DÍA DE DIFUNTOS

Ahora que han pasado nueve meses
y que el invierno quedó atrás,
en estas tardes últimas de julio
pesarosas, cuando la luz color de acero
nos refugia en los sótanos,
quiero yo recordar un cielo azul de octubre
puro y profundo de Madrid,
y un día dedicado a la mejor memoria
de aquellos, cuyas vidas
son materia común,
sustancia y fundamento de nuestra libertad
más allá de los limites estrechos de la muerte.

Éramos unos cuantos
intelectuales, compañeros jóvenes,
los que aquella mañana lentamente avanzábamos
entre la multitud, camino de los cementerios,
pasada ya la hilera de los cobrizos álamos
y los desmontes suavizados
por el continuo régimen de lluvias,
hacia el lugar en que la carretera
recta apuntaba al corazón del campo.

Donde nos detuvimos,
junto a las grandes verjas historiadas,
a mirar el gran río de la gente
por la avenida al sol, que se arremolinaba
para luego perderse en los rincones
de la Sacramental, entre cipreses.
Aunque nosotros íbamos más lejos.

Sólo unos pocos pasos
nos separaban ya.
Y entramos uno a uno, en silencio,
como si aquel recinto
despertase en nosotros un sentimiento raro,
mezcla de soledad,
de solidaridad, que no recuerdo nunca
haber sentido en otro cementerio.

Porque no éramos muchos, es verdad,
en el campo sin cruces donde unos españoles
duermen aparte el sueño,
encomendados sólo a la esperanza humana,
a la memoria y las generaciones,
pero algo había uniéndonos a todos.

ALL SAINTS DAY

Now that it's been nine months
and winter's behind us,
in these glum afternoons at the end
of July when we lie low
in steel-tinged underground light,
I want to keep alive a clear,
deep-blue October sky in Madrid
and a day set aside to better remember
those whose lives
are a common ground,
core and base of our freedom
far beyond death's narrow confines.

We were just a few
thinkers, young companions
slowly pushing on through the crowd
that morning on the way to the cemeteries,
past the row of coppery poplars
and cleared fields made spongy
by a steady diet of rain
toward that place where the highway
points straight to the graveyard's heart.

Where we stopped off,
by the big ornate gates,
to watch the wide river of people
whirl along the sunny avenue
later to be lost among cypresses
in nooks of the Sacramental Cemetery.
Yet we were heading much farther.

Then we were
just a few steps away.
Silently we slipped in, one by one,
as if that sealed-off area
stirred a strange sense in us,
alloy of loneliness
and solidarity I don't remember
ever having felt in any other cemetery.

Because we really weren't many
among the crossless tombs where a few
Spaniards sleep a separate dream
dedicated only to human hope,
memory and future generations
but something linked us to everyone.

Algo vivo y humilde después de tantos años,
como aquellas cadenas de claveles rojos
dejadas por el pueblo
al pie del monumento a Pablo Iglesias,
como aquellas palabras:
te acuerdas, María, cuántas banderas . . .
dichas en voz muy baja por una voz de hombre.
Y era la afirmación de aquel pasado,
la configuración de un porvenir
distinto y más hermoso.
                              Bajo la luz, al aire
libre del extrarradio, allí permanecíamos
no sé cuántos instantes
una pequeña multitud callada.

Ahora que han pasado nueve meses,
a vosotros, paisanos
del pueblo de Madrid, intelectuales,
pintores y escritores amigos,
mientras fuera oscurece imperceptiblemente,
quiero yo recordaros.
Porque pienso que en todos la imagen de aquel día,
la visión de aquel sol
y de aquella cabeza de español yacente
vivirán como un símbolo, como una invocación
apasionada hacia el futuro, en los momentos malos.

After all these years, something humble
and alive as those daisy-chained
red carnations placed by workers
under the monument to Pablo Iglesias,
as those words:
"Remember, María, how many flags . . . "
whispered in a man's lowered voice.
And it acknowledged that past,
the shape of a different,
more beautiful time to come.
                              There in the light,
in the wide outdoors of the outskirts
we stayed I don't know how many minutes,
a small, speechless multitude.

Now that it's been nine months,
while outside it gradually
grows gloomier, I want you
to remember this,
natives of Madrid's streets,
my thinker, painter and writer friends.
Because I imagine for all of us
that day's impression, that sun's vision
and the head of that Spaniard laid to rest
will live on as a symbol, as a passionate
call to the future, in the worst of times.

AÑOS TRIUNFALES

. . . y la más hermosa
sonríe al más fiero de los vencedores.

– Rubén Darío

Media España ocupaba España entera
con la vulgaridad, con el desprecio
total de que es capaz, frente al vencido,
un intratable pueblo de cabreros.

Barcelona y Madrid eran algo humillado.
Como una casa sucia, donde la gente es vieja,
la ciudad parecía más oscura
y los Metros olían a miseria.

Con luz de atardecer, sobresaltada y triste,
se salia a las calles de un invierno
poblado de infelices gabardinas
a la deriva, bajo el viento.

Y pasaban figuras mal vestidas
de mujeres, cruzando como sombras,
solitarias mujeres adiestradas
— viudas, hijas o esposas —

en los modos peores de ganar la vida
y suplir a sus hombres. Por la noche,
las más hermosas sonreían
a los más insolentes de los vencedores.

YEARS OF TRIUMPH

*. . . and the most beautiful
smiles at the cruelest of the conquerors.*

– Rubén Darío

Half of Spain occupied all of Spain
with the vulgarity and complete disdain
only an unruly nation of rednecks
could show the defeated.

Barcelona and Madrid were put to shame.
Like a dingy household of the old,
the city seemed much dimmer
and subways reeked of poverty.

With the sad, cringing light of dusk,
people would spill out into streets
of a winter inhabited by miserable
raincoats drifting along in the wind.

And crossing like shadows, the forms
of shabbily clad women would glide by —
widows, daughters or wives —
solitary women skilled

in the lowest ways of making money
and providing for their men. At night
the most beautiful would smile
at the most arrogant of the conquerors.

DURANTE LA INVASIÓN

Sobre el mantel, abierto, está el periódico
de la mañana. Brilla el sol en los vasos.
Almuerzo en el pequeño restaurante,
un día de trabajo.

Callamos casi todos. Alguien habla en voz vaga
— y son conversaciones con la especial tristeza
de las cosas que siempre suceden
y que no acaban nunca, o acaban en desgracia.

Yo pienso que a estas horas amanece en la Ciénaga,
que todo está indeciso, que no cesa el combate,
y busco en las noticias un poco de esperanza
que no venga de Miami.

Oh Cuba en el veloz amanecer del trópico,
cuando el sol no calienta y está el aire claro:
que tu tierra dé tanques y que tu cielo roto
sea gris de las alas de tus aeroplanos!

Contigo están las gentes de la caña de azúcar,
el hombre del tranvía, los de los restaurantes,
y todos cuantos hoy buscamos en el mundo
un poco de esperanza que no venga de Miami.

DURING THE INVASION

The morning paper lies open on
the tablecloth. Sunlight glints in
the glasses. A workday, I eat lunch
in a small restaurant.

Most of us fall silent. Someone's speaking
in indistinct tones — talk especially saddened
by how things are always happening
and drag on forever, or end in disaster.

I imagine it's dawn around now in the Ciénaga,
everything uncertain, no pause in the fighting
and in the news I search for a little hope
that doesn't come from Miami.

O Cuba in the fleeting tropical dawn
when the sun's not hot and the air clear:
may your land sprout tanks, your shattered sky
turn gray with the wings of your planes!

The sugar-cane people, the streetcar man,
the folks in restaurants are with you
and all of us today who search the world over
for a little hope that doesn't come from Miami.

RUINAS DEL TERCER REICH

Todo pasó como él imaginara,
allá en el frente de Smolensk.
Y tú has envejecido — aunque sonrías
wie einst, Lili Marlen.

Nimbado por la niebla, igual que entonces,
surge ante mí tu rostro encantador
contra un fondo de carros de combate
y de cruces gamadas en la Place Vendôme.

En la barra del bar — ante una copa — ,
plantada como cimbel,
obscenamente tú sonríes.
A quién, Lili Marlen?

Por los rusos vencido y por los años,
aún el irritado corazón
te pide guerra. Y en las horas últimas
de soledad y alcohol,

enfurecida y flaca, con las uñas
destrozas el pespunte de tu guante negro,
tu viejo guante de manopla negro
con que al partir dijiste adiós.

RUINS OF THE THIRD REICH

Everything turned out how he imagined,
there on the Smolensk front.
And you've grown old — even if you smile
wie einst, Lili Marlene.

Haloed by fog, the same as then,
your bewitching face rises before me
against a backdrop of combat vehicles
and swastikas in the Place Vendôme.

Propped like a decoy — in front of a drink —
at the bar of a café
you smile lewdly.
At whom, Lili Marlene?

Crushed by the Russians, by the years,
your peevish heart still
wants war. And in the final
hours of booze and solitude

rail-thin and rabid, your fingernails
unravel your black glove's stitches,
the old raven brocade gauntlet that,
walking out, you raise to wave goodbye.

INTENTO FORMULAR MI EXPERIENCIA DE LA GUERRA

Fueron, posiblemente,
los años más felices de mi vida,
y no es extraño, puesto que a fin de cuentas
no tenía los diez.

Las víctimas más tristes de la guerra
los niños son, se dice.
Pero también es cierto que es una bestia el niño:
si le perdona la brutalidad
de los mayores, él sabe aprovecharla,
y vive más que nadie
en ese mundo demasiado simple,
tan parecido al suyo.

Para empezar, la guerra
fue conocer los páramos con viento,
los sembrados de gleba pegajosa
y las tardes de azul, celestes y algo pálidas,
con los montes de nieve sonrosada a lo lejos.
Mi amor por los inviernos mesetarios
es una consecuencia
de que hubiera en España casi un millón de muertos.

A salvo en los pinares
— pinares de la Mesa, del Rosal, del Jinete! — ,
el miedo y el desorden de los primeros días
eran algo borroso, con esa irrealidad
de los momentos demasiado intensos.
Y Segovia parecía remota
como una gran ciudad, era ya casi el frente
— o por lo menos un lugar heroico,
un sitio con tenientes de brazo en cabestrillo
que nos emocionaba visitar: la guerra
quedaba allí al alcance de los niños
tal y como la quieren.
A la vuelta, de paso por el puente Uñés,
buscábamos la arena removida
donde estaban, sabíamos, los cinco fusilados.
Luego la lluvia los desenterró,
los llevó río abajo.

Y me acuerdo también de una excursión a Coca,
que era el pueblo de al lado,
una de esas mañanas que la luz
es aún, en el aire, relámpago de escarcha,
pero que anuncian ya la primavera.

I TRY TO GIVE SHAPE TO MY WAR EXPERIENCE

They were possibly
the happiest years of my life
and that's not odd, since in the end
I wasn't even ten.

Children, they say,
are war's most tragic victims.
But it's also true children are monsters:
if adult brutality spares them
they know how to make the most of it
and more than anyone else
are at home in that too simple
world so much like their own.

To begin with, the war
was getting to know windy wastelands,
furrowed fields fresh with sticky clods
and palish, sky-blue afternoons
with rose-tinted snow on faraway mountains.
My love for mesa-land winters
is a direct result
of the almost million dead in Spain.

Out of harm's way in pine forests —
pine forests of Mesa, Rosal, Jinete! —
the first days of fear and confusion
somehow blurred into that dreamstate
of moments lived too deeply.
And Segovia seemed as far off as a big city
but by then was almost the front —
or a least a heroic place
full of lieutenants in arm slings
that it thrilled us to visit: the war,
right there within children's reach,
was just where they wanted it.
On the way home, going by the Uñés bridge,
we combed the freshly turned sand where,
we just knew, five shot men lay buried.
Rain later washed them out
and dragged them downstream.

And I also remember an outing to Coca,
the town nextdoor to ours,
on one of those mornings when light
is still a flash of white frost
in the air, though hinting of spring.

Mi recuerdo, muy vago, es sólo una imagen,
una nítida imagen de la felicidad
retratada en un cielo
hacia el que se apresura la torre de la iglesia,
entre un nimbo de pájaros.
Y los mismos discursos, los gritos, las canciones
eran como promesas de otro tiempo mejor,
nos ofrecían
un billete de vuelta al siglo diez y seis.
Qué niño no lo acepta?

Cuando por fin volvimos
a Barcelona, me quedó unos meses
la nostalgia de aquello, pero me acostumbré.
Quien me conoce ahora
dirá que mi experiencia
nada tiene que ver con mis ideas,
y es verdad. Mis ideas de la guerra cambiaron
después, mucho después
de que hubiera empezado la postguerra.

My memory is pretty fuzzy, just an image,
a glowing image of happiness
crayoned above in a sky
the church tower is zooming toward
amid a halo of birds.
And those very speeches, shouts and songs
were like promises of another, better time
offering us
a round-trip to the sixteenth century.
What child would turn it down?

When we finally got back
to Barcelona, a longing for all that
lasted a few months but I got over it.
People who know me now
would say my experience
and my ideas have nothing in common
and they're right. My thoughts on the war
matured later, a long time after
the postwar era had begun.

ELEGÍA Y RECUERDO DE LA CANCIÓN FRANCESA

> *C'est une chanson*
> *qui nous ressemble.*
>
> – Kosma y Prévert:
> "Les feuilles mortes"

Os acordáis: Europa estaba en ruinas.
Todo un mundo de imágenes me queda de aquel tiempo
descoloridas, hiriéndome los ojos
con los escombros de los bombardeos.
En España la gente se apretaba en los cines
y no existía la calefacción.

Era la paz — después de tanta sangre —
que llegaba harapienta, como la conocimos
los españoles durante cinco años.
Y todo un continente empobrecido,
carcomido de historia y de mercado negro,
de repente nos fue más familiar.

¡Estampas de la Europa de postguerra
que parecen mojadas en lluvia silenciosa,
ciudades grises adonde llega un tren
sucio de refugiados: cuántas cosas
de nuestra historia próxima trajisteis, despertando
la esperanza en España, y el temor!

Hasta el aire de entonces parecía
que estuviera suspenso, como si preguntara,
y en las viejas tabernas de barrio
los vencidos hablaban en voz baja . . .
Nosotros, los más jóvenes, como siempre esperábamos
algo definitivo y general.

Y fue en aquel momento, justamente
en aquellos momentos de miedo y esperanzas
— tan irreales, ay — que apareciste,
oh rosa de lo sórdido, manchada
creación de los hombres, arisca, vil y bella
canción francesa de mi juventud!

Eras lo no esperado que se impone
a la imaginación, porque es así la vida,
tú que cantabas la heroicidad canalla,
el estallido de las rebeldías
igual que llamaradas, y el miedo a dormir solo,
la intensidad que aflige al corazón.

ELEGY IN MEMORY OF THE FRENCH SONG

C'est une chanson
qui nous ressemble.

– Kosma and Prévert,
"Les feuilles mortes"

Most of you remember: Europe was in ruins.
A whole world of bleached-out images
from that time haunts me, my eyes smarting
from the jagged debris left by the bombs.
In Spain people huddled together at movies
and heating simply didn't exist.

After so much bloodshed, it was a peace
that dawned in dirty rags, just as we
Spaniards had known it for five years.
And an entire penniless continent,
wormy with history and the black market,
suddenly looked much more like home.

Prints of postwar Europe
that seem soaked in silent rain,
drab cities where a filthy train
of refugees pulls in: how much
of our own recent history you brought,
stirring up hope in Spain, and fear!

Even the air in those days seemed
somehow arrested, as if asking a question
and in old neighborhood bars
the defeated spoke in whispers . . . .
As usual we, the youngest, were waiting
for a definitive and universal something.

And it was at that moment, exactly
in those times of hope and fear —
ah, so unbelievable — you came along,
O licentious rose, tarnished human
creation, surly, base and beautiful,
French song of my youth.

You were a bolt from the blue that takes
hold of the imagination, for such is life.
You who sang of cutthroat courage,
the lashing out of rebellions
like flash fires, the fear of sleeping alone,
the white heat that breaks your heart.

Cuánto enseguida te quisimos todos!
En tu mundo de noches, con el chico y la chica
entrelazados, de pie en un quicio oscuro,
en la sordina de tus melodías,
un eco de nosotros resonaba exaltándonos
con la nostalgia de la rebelión.

Y todavía, en la alta noche, solo,
con el vaso en la mano, cuando pienso en mi vida,
otra vez más *sans faire du bruit* tus músicas
suenan en la memoria, como una despedida:
parece que fue ayer y algo ha cambiado.
Hoy no esperamos la revolución.

Desvencijada Europa de postguerra
con la luna asomando tras las ventanas rotas,
Europa anterior al milagro alemán,
imagen de mi vida, melancólica!
Nosotros, los de entonces, ya no somos los mismos,
aunque a veces nos guste una canción.

How much we all loved you right away!
In your night world, with the boy and girl
wrapped around each other in some dark doorway,
in your melodies' muted tones
we caught an echo of ourselves,
sweeping us up in a longing to rebel.

And even now, late at night, alone
with a drink in hand, when I think of my life
your melodies swell again in my memory
sans faire de bruit, like a goodbye.
It seems like yesterday but something's missing.
We're not waiting for the revolution any more.

Crumbling postwar Europe with the moon
looming through broken windowpanes,
Europe before the German miracle,
melancholy image of my life!
We from back then are no longer the same,
although occasionally we like a good song.

EL JUEGO DE HACER VERSOS

El juego de hacer versos
— que no es un juego — es algo
parecido en principio
al placer solitario.

Con la primera muda,
en los años nostálgicos
de nuestra adolescencia,
a escribir empezamos.

Y son nuestros poemas
del todo imaginarios
— demasiado inexpertos
ni siquiera plagiamos —

porque la Poesía
es un ángel abstracto
y, como todos ellos,
predispuesto a halagarnos.

El arte es otra cosa
distinta. El resultado
de mucha vocación
y un poco de trabajo.

Aprender a pensar
en renglones contados
— y no en los sentimientos
con que nos exaltábamos — ,

tratar con el idioma
como si fuera mágico
es un buen ejercicio,
que llega a emborracharnos.

Luego está el instrumento
en su punto afinado:
la mejor poesía
es el Verbo hecho tango.

Y los poemas son
un modo que adoptamos
para que nos entiendan
y que nos entendamos.

Lo que importa explicar
es la vida, los rasgos
de su filantropía,
las noches de sus sábados.

THE POEM-WRITING GAME

The poem-writing game —
it's no game — starts out
seeming something like
the solitary pleasure.

We begin to scribble
with the change of skin
in the times of longing
of our teenage years.

And our poems are
completely "poetic" —
too inept even to be
cribbed from a text —

because poetry flatters,
is an abstract angel
and like all of its feather
tends to sweet-talk us.

Art is something else
altogether. Net result
of a lot of calling
and a bit of sweat.

To learn to think
in regular lines —
and not in the feelings
that swept us along —

to deal with words
as if they were magic
is not bad practice
but leaves us reeling.

Then there's the tool
sharpened to a point:
in the very best poetry
the Word becomes a tango.

And poems are how
we choose to be
understood by others
and by ourselves.

What's essential
to explain is life,
its philanthropic aspects
and its Saturday nights.

La manera que tiene
sobre todo en verano
de ser un paraíso.
Aunque, de cuando en cuando,

si alguna de esas noches
que las carga el diablo
uno piensa en la historia
de estos últimos años,

si piensa en esta vida
que nos hace pedazos
de madera podrida,
perdida en un naufragio,

la conciencia le pesa
— por estar intentando
persuadirse en secreto
de que aún es honrado.

El juego de hacer versos,
que no es un juego, es algo
que acaba pareciéndose
al vicio solitario.

That certain way it has,
especially during summer,
of turning into paradise.
Although if anyone considers

on one of those rare nights
when all hell breaks loose
the history of what's happened
in these past few years

if he considers how life
cracks us into splinters
of water-logged timber
scattered in a shipwreck,

his conscience bogs down
with the sneaky way
he tries to delude himself
that he's still honest.

The poem-writing game,
which is no game, ends up
seeming something like
the solitary vice.

PANDÉMICA Y CELESTE

quam magnus numerus Libyssae arenae

. . .

aut quam sidera multa, cum tacet nox,
furtiuos hominum uident amores.

— Catulo, VII

Imagínate ahora que tú y yo
muy tarde ya en la noche
hablemos hombre a hombre, finalmente.
Imagínatelo,
en una de esas noches memorables
de rara comunión, con la botella
medio vacía, los ceniceros sucios,
y después de agotado el tema de la vida.
Que te voy a enseñar un corazón,
un corazón infiel,
desnudo de cintura para abajo,
hipócrita lector — *mon semblable,* — *mon frère!*

Porque no es la impaciencia del buscador de orgasmo
quien me tira del cuerpo hacia otros cuerpos
a ser posible jóvenes:
yo persigo también el dulce amor,
el tierno amor para dormir al lado
y que alegre mi cama al despertarse,
cercano como un pájaro.
¡Si yo no puedo desnudarme nunca,
si jamás he podido entrar en unos brazos
sin sentir — aunque sea nada más que un momento —
igual deslumbramiento que a los veinte años!

Para saber de amor, para aprenderle,
haber estado solo es necesario.
Y es necesario en cuatrocientas noches
— con cuatrocientos cuerpos diferentes —
haber hecho el amor. Que sus misterios,
como dijo el poeta, son del alma,
pero un cuerpo es el libro en que se leen.

Y por eso me alegro de haberme revolcado
sobre la arena gruesa, los dos medio vestidos,
mientras buscaba ese tendón del hombro.
Me conmueve el recuerdo de tantas ocasiones . . .
Aquella carretera de montaña
y los bien empleados abrazos furtivos
y el instante indefenso, de pie, tras el frenazo,

PANDEMIC AND CELESTE

quam magnus numerus Libyssae arenae

.   .   .

aut quam sidera multa, cum tacet nox,
furtiuos hominum uident amores.

– Catullus, VII

Now just imagine very late at night
you and I are talking
man-to-man at last.
Picture it
on one of those unforgetable nights
of rare communion, with the bottle
half-empty, ashtrays overflowing
and the subject of life more than worn out.
What I'm going to show you is a heart,
an unfaithful one
naked from the waist down,
hypocrite reader — *mon semblable* — *mon frère!*

Because it's not the haste of someone cruising
for orgasms that flings me from my own body
toward other bodies, young if at all possible:
I also stalk sweet love,
the tender kind to sleep at my side
and make my bed a joy to wake up in
like a bird nearby.
No, I never can take off my clothes,
never can enter another's arms
without feeling — if just for a moment —
as dazzled as I did at twenty!

To know love, to learn about it,
it's necessary to have been alone.
And it's necessary to have made love
on four hundred nights — with four hundred
different bodies. Its mysteries,
as the poet said, are of the soul
but a body is the book in which they are read.

And that's why I'm happy to have rolled around
on the coarse sand, both of us half-dressed,
while I felt for that brawn in the shoulder.
I'm moved remembering so many instances . . . .
That mountain road and the carefully managed
hidden gropings and the vulnerable moment,
after slamming on the brakes, standing

pegados a la tapia, cegados por las luces.
O aquel atardecer cerca del río
desnudos y riéndonos, de yedra coronados.
O aquel portal en Roma — en via del Babuino.
Y recuerdos de caras y ciudades
apenas conocidas, de cuerpos entrevistos,
de escaleras sin luz, de camarotes,
de bares, de pasajes desiertos, de prostíbulos,
y de infinitas casetas de baños,
de fosos de un castillo.
Recuerdos de vosotras, sobre todo,
oh noches en hoteles de una noche,
definitivas noches en pensiones sórdidas,
en cuartos recién fríos,
noches que devolvéis a vuestros huéspedes
un olvidado sabor a sí mismos!
La historia en cuerpo y alma, como una imagen rota,
de la langueur goutée à ce mal d'être deux.
Sin despreciar
— alegres como fiesta entre semana —
las experiencias de promiscuidad.

Aunque sepa que nada me valdrían
trabajos de amor disperso
si no existiese el verdadero amor.
Mi amor,
              íntegra imagen de mi vida,
sol de las noches mismas que le robo.

Su juventud, la mía,
— música de mi fondo —
sonríe aún en la imprecisa gracia
de cada cuerpo joven,
en cada encuentro anónimo,
iluminándolo. Dándole un alma.
Y no hay muslos hermosos
que no me hagan pensar en sus hermosos muslos
cuando nos conocimos, antes de ir a la cama.

Ni pasión de una noche de dormida
que pueda compararla
con la pasión que da el conocimiento,
los años de experiencia
de nuestro amor.
                        Porque en amor también
es importante el tiempo,
y dulce, de algún modo,
verificar con mano melancólica
su perceptible paso por un cuerpo

78

glued to the embankment, blinded by light.
Or that late afternoon by the river,
naked, laughing and crowned with ivy.
Or that doorway in Rome — on Via del Babuino.
And memories of faces and cities
barely known, bodies only glimpsed,
of unlit stairwells, ship cabins,
of bars, deserted passageways, whorehouses
and endless seaside changing booths,
of castle moats.
Especially memories of all of you,
O nights in one-night cheap hotels,
definitive nights in seedy rented rooms,
in rooms just vacated,
nights that give back to your guests
the forgotten smell of themselves.
Like a broken image, the story in body and soul
de la langueur goutée à ce mal d'être deux.
Without putting down —
festive as a weekday holiday —
the pleasures of sleeping around.

Although I suspect my love's labors scattered
wouldn't be worth much
if it weren't for real love.
My love,
         whole image of my life,
sun of the same nights I steal.

His youth, mine —
music from the core of me —
still smiles in the fumbling grace
of each young body,
of each anonymous encounter,
illuminating it. Giving it soul.
And there are no beautiful thighs
that don't recall his beautiful thighs
when we first met, before going to bed.

Not even the passion of a one-night stand
can compare with the passion
that comes from the understanding,
the years of experience
of our love.
         For with love
time is also important and
in some ways it's rather sweet
to trace with a melancholy hand
its perceptible path across the body —

— mientras que basta un gesto familiar
en los labios,
o la ligera palpitación de un miembro,
para hacerme sentir la maravilla
de aquella gracia antigua,
fugaz como un reflejo.

Sobre su piel borrosa,
cuando pasen más años y al final estemos,
quiero aplastar los labios invocando
la imagen de su cuerpo
y de todos los cuerpos que una vez amé
aunque fuese un instante, deshechos por el tiempo.
Para pedir la fuerza de poder vivir
sin belleza, sin fuerza y sin deseo,
mientras seguimos juntos
hasta morir en paz, los dos,
como dicen que mueren los que han amado mucho.

while a familiar expression on the lips
or a limb's slight pulsing
is enough to make me marvel
at that classic grace
fleeting as a reflection.

After more years slide by, when we reach the end,
I want to press my lips
against his bleary skin
calling up the image of his body
and of all those bodies blotted out by time
that I loved just once, if only for a moment.
To ask for the courage to go on living
without beauty, without strength or desire
while we remain together
until both of us die in peace,
as it's said those die who have loved so much.

III

from
Poemas póstumos (1968):

Posthumous Poems

CONTRA JAIME GIL DE BIEDMA

De qué sirve, quisiera yo saber, cambiar de piso,
dejar atrás un sótano más negro
que mi reputación — y ya es decir — ,
poner visillos blancos
y tomar criada,
renunciar a la vida de bohemio,
si vienes luego tú, pelmazo,
embarazoso huésped, memo vestido con mis trajes,
zángano de colmena, inútil, cacaseno,
con tus manos lavadas,
a comer en mi plato y a ensuciar la casa?

Te acompañan las barras de los bares
últimos de la noche, los chulos, las floristas,
las calles muertas de la madrugada
y los ascensores de luz amarilla
cuando llegas, borracho,
y te paras a verte en el espejo
la cara destruida,
con ojos todavía violentos
que no quieres cerrar. Y si te increpo,
te ríes, me recuerdas el pasado
y dices que envejezco.

Podría recordarte que ya no tienes gracia.
Que tu estilo casual y que tu desenfado
resultan truculentos
cuando se tienen más de treinta años,
y que tu encantadora
sonrisa de muchacho soñoliento
— seguro de gustar — es un resto penoso,
un intento patético.
Mientras que tú me miras con tus ojos
de verdadero huérfano, y me lloras
y me prometes ya no hacerlo.

Si no fueses tan puta!
Y si yo no supiese, hace ya tiempo,
que tú eres fuerte cuando yo soy débil
y que eres débil cuando me enfurezco . . .
De tus regresos guardo una impresión confusa
de pánico, de pena y descontento,
y la desesperanza
y la impaciencia y el resentimiento
de volver a sufrir, otra vez más,
la humillación imperdonable

AGAINST JAIME GIL DE BIEDMA

What good, I'd like to know, is it to move,
to leave behind a basement even murkier
than my reputation — which is saying a lot —
to hang white lace curtains,
hire a maid
and turn away from my bohemian days
only to have you, big galoot,
bungling boarder absurdly dolled up in my suits,
idle drone, idiotic and in the way,
to have you turn up with hands just washed
to take bites off my plate and mess up the place?

Hustlers and florists keep you company
on the stools of the last bars to close
and at dawn so do the empty streets
and the yellow elevator light
when you stumble home drunk
and stop to study the ravages
of your face in the mirror
with the still-crazed eyes
you refuse to shut. And if I say a word,
you laugh me off, remind me of the past
and say I'm just getting old.

I could remind you that you're not so charming anymore.
That your sporty style, your cool
turned cruel
after you hit thirty.
And that your winning smile
of a dreamy kid —
sure to please — is a labored leftover,
a pretty sad try.
Meanwhile you gaze at me with your trueblue
orphan's eyes and you cry on my shoulder
and promise me not to do it anymore.

If only you weren't such a little whore!
And if I didn't know, as I have for years,
that you take over when I give in
and you grow faint when I rage . . . .
The impression I get when you come home
is a jumble of panic, hurt and disgust,
of depression
and impatience and resentment
at coming back to endure, one more time,
the inexcusable shame

de la excesiva intimidad.

A duras penas te llevaré a la cama,
como quien va al infierno
para dormir contigo.
Muriendo a cada paso de impotencia,
tropezando con muebles
a tientas, cruzaremos el piso
torpemente abrazados, vacilando
de alcohol y de sollozos reprimidos.
Oh innoble servidumbre de amar seres humanos,
y la más innoble
que es amarse a sí mismo!

of being far to close to me.

I'll have a terrible time putting you to bed
and you're hell
to sleep with.
Swooning at every limp step
and stumbling against furniture
we'll grope our way through the apartment
in a clumsy embrace, staggering
from drink and choked-back sobs.
O what lowdown drudgery to love another
and the lowest
is to love yourself!

NOSTALGIE DE LA BOUE

Nuevas disposiciones de la noche,
sórdidos ejercicios al dictado, lecciones del deseo
que yo aprendí, pirata,
oh joven pirata de los ojos azules.

En calles resonantes la oscuridad tenía
todavía la misma espesura total
que recuerdo en mi infancia.
Y dramáticas sombras, revestidas
con el prestigio de la prostitución,
a mi lado venían de un infierno
grasiento y sofocante como un cuarto de máquinas.

¡Largas últimas horas,
en mundos amueblados
con deslustrada loza sanitaria
y cortinas manchadas de permanganato!
Como un operario que pule una pieza,
como un afilador,
fornicar poco a poco mordiéndome los labios.

Y sentirse morir por cada pelo
de gusto, y hacer daño.

La luz amarillenta, la escalera
estremecida toda de susurros, mis pasos,
eran aún una prolongación
que me exaltaba,
lo mismo que el olor en las manos
— o que al salir el frío de la madrugada, intenso
como el recuerdo de una sensación.

NOSTALGIE DE LA BOUE

New inclinations of the night,
lewd exercises by rote, lessons in lust
that I mastered, pirate,
O young blue-eyed pirate.

In echoing streets darkness
was still the same thick liquid
I remember as a child.
And dramatic shadows draped
with the classic spell of prostitution
would sidle up beside me from a hell
greasy and airless as an engire room.

All the endless
late-night hours in worlds furnished
with tarnished bathroom porcelain
and curtains stained purple with permanganate!
Like a mechanic, like a grinder
polishing a piece,
biting my lip, I would fornicate carefully,

feel myself die for each drop
of pleasure, making it hurt.

The ocherous glow, the stairwell buzzing
all over with whispers, my footsteps descending
would draw it out even farther
and drive me wild,
same as the smell still on my hands —
or slipping out into the early morning cold, sharp
as that feeling, remembered.

UN CUERPO ES EL MEJOR AMIGO DEL HOMBRE

Las horas no han pasado, todavía,
y está mañana lejos igual a un arrecife
que apenas yo distingo.

              Tú no sientes
cómo el tiempo se adensa en esta habitación
con la luz encendida, como está fuera el frío
lamiendo los cristales . . . Qué deprisa,
en mi cama esta noche, animalito,
con la simple nobleza de la necesidad,
mientras que te miraba, te quedaste dormido.

Así pues, buenas noches.
                  Ese país tranquilo
cuyos contornos son los de tu cuerpo
da ganas de morir recordando la vida,
o de seguir despierto
— cansado y excitado — hasta el amanecer.

A solas con la edad, mientras tú duermes
como quien no ha leído nunca un libro,
pequeño animalito: ser humano
— más franco que en mis brazos — ,
por lo desconocido.

A BODY IS A MAN'S BEST FRIEND

The hours aren't over, not yet,
and tomorrow's as far away
as a reef I can barely make out.

                    You don't notice
how thickly time is growing in this room
with the lamp glowing, how the chill
is outside licking at the windowpanes . . . .
How quickly, little creature, you fell asleep
in my bed tonight with the easy nobility
born of necessity while I studied you.

So good night then.
                    That quiet country
bordered by your body's contours
makes me want to die remembering life,
or to stay up —
exhausted and excited — until dawn.

Alone with old age while you sleep
like someone who's never read a book,
funny little creature: so human —
much more sincere than in my arms —
because a perfect stranger.

DEL AÑO MALO

Diciembre es esta imagen
de la lluvia cayendo con rumor de tren,
con un olor difuso a carbonilla y campo.
Diciembre es un jardín, es una plaza
hundida en la ciudad,
al final de una noche,
y la visión en fuga de unos soportales.

Y los ojos inmensos
— tizones agrandados —
en la cara morena de una cría
temblando igual que un gorrión mojado.
En la mano sostiene unos zapatos rojos,
elegantes, flamantes como un pájaro exótico.

El cielo es negro y gris
y rosa en sus extremos,
la luz de las farolas un resto amarillento.
Bajo un golpe de lluvia, llorando, yo atravieso,
innoble como un trapo, mojado hasta los cuernos.

THE BAD YEAR

December: this image of rain falling
with the moan of a passing train
and a pervasive smell of coaldust and fields.
December is a garden, is a square
sunken inside the city
at the end of the night
and archways narrowing into the distance.

And the immense eyes —
wide open branding irons —
in the face of a dark-skinned girl
trembling like a soaked sparrow.
In her hand she holds out fancy shoes
flaming red as a tropical bird.

The sooty gray sky
bleeds rose around the edges,
the streetlamps an amber afterglow.
Weeping, I cross through a downpour,
common as a dishrag, wet to the gills.

HA VENIDO A ESA HORA

No vive en este barrio.
No conoce las tiendas.
No conoce a las gentes
que se afanan en ellas.
No sabe a lo que vino.
No compra aquí la prensa.
Recuerda las esquinas
que los perros recuerdan.

Ventanas encendidas
le agrandan la tristeza.
Corazón transeúnte,
junto a las casas nuevas
camina vacilando,
como un hombre a quien llevan.
El viento del suburbio
se le enreda en las piernas.

La calle como entonces.
Como entonces ajena.
Y el aire oscurecido
la noche que se acerca.
Cuando dobla la esquina
y aprieta el paso, sueña
que el tiempo no ha cambiado,
jugando a que regresa.

Luego pasa de largo,
y piensa: fue una época.

HE'S COME TO THAT TIME

He doesn't live in this neighborhood.
He doesn't shop in its stores.
He doesn't know these people
who slave away in them.
He's not sure why he came.
He doesn't buy the paper here.
He remembers the corners
the way dogs do.

Brightly lit windows
swell his sadness.
Pedestrian heart,
he zigzags his way
next to the new houses
like someone dragged along.
The suburban wind
has him tangled by the legs.

The street as it was.
Strange as it was.
And the air shadowy,
night inching closer.
When he turns the corner
he walks faster, daydreaming
that times haven't changed,
any day they'll be back.

Later he passes by without stopping
and thinks:

                  another closed chapter.

NO VOLVERÉ A SER JOVEN

Que la vida iba en serio
uno lo empieza a comprender más tarde
— como todos los jóvenes, yo vine
a llevarme la vida por delante.

Dejar huella quería
y marcharme entre aplausos
— envejecer, morir, eran tan sólo
las dimensiones del teatro.

Pero ha pasado el tiempo
y la verdad desagradable asoma:
envejecer, morir,
es el único argumento de la obra.

I SHALL NEVER BE YOUNG AGAIN

Then, later, you begin to see
that life is a serious business —
like everyone young I arrived
on the scene, my life before me.

I only wanted to make my mark
then exit stage-left to applause —
growing old and dying were just
so many backdrops and props.

But the years have raced by and
the terrible truth looms larger:
the only plot this play has got
is growing old and then dying.

Dancing in Athens, 1966

Recovering from tuberculosis in the garden of the family house,
Nava de la Asunción, August 1956

DESPUÉS DE LA MUERTE DE JAIME GIL DE BIEDMA

En el jardín, leyendo,
la sombra de la casa me oscurece las páginas
y el frío repentino de final de agosto
hace que piense en ti.

El jardín y la casa cercana
donde pían los pájaros en las enredaderas,
una tarde de agosto, cuando va a oscurecer
y se tiene aún el libro en la mano,
eran, me acuerdo, símbolo tuyo de la muerte.
Ojalá en el infierno
de tus últimos días te diera esta visión
un poco de dulzura, aunque no lo creo.

En paz al fin conmigo,
puedo ya recordarte
no en las horas horribles, sino aquí
en el verano del año pasado,
cuando agolpadamente
— tantos meses borradas —
regresan las imágenes felices
traídas por tu imagen de la muerte . . .
Agosto en el jardín, a pleno día.

Vasos de vino blanco
dejados en la hierba, cerca de la piscina,
calor bajo los árboles. Y voces
que gritan nombres.
                   Ángel.
Juan. María Rosa. Marcelino. Joaquina
— Joaquina de pechitos de manzana.
Tú volvías riendo del teléfono
anunciando más gente que venía:
te recuerdo correr,
la apagada explosión de tu cuerpo en el agua.

Y las noches también de libertad completa
en la casa espaciosa, toda para nosotros
lo mismo que un convento abandonado,
y la nostalgia de puertas secretas,
aquel correr por las habitaciones,
buscar en los armarios
y divertirse en la alternancia
de desnudo y disfraz, desempolvando
batines, botas altas y calzones,
arbitrarias escenas,

AFTER THE DEATH OF JAIME GIL DE BIEDMA

Reading in the garden:
the house's shadow falls across my pages
and the abrupt end-of-August chill
makes me think of you.

The garden and nearby house
where birds chirp in tendriled vines
on a late August afternoon edging
toward evening, with a book still in hand:
this, I recall, was your symbol for death.
I hope to God in the hell
of your final days this vision lent you
some solace, though I doubt it.

At peace with myself at last,
now I can remember you
not in the horrendous hours
but here, last summer,
whose happy images rush —
erased for so many months —
crowding back, brought on
by your image for death . . . .
The August garden, in broad daylight.

Glasses of white wine
left in the grass near the pool,
heat under the trees. And voices
shouting names.
                        Ángel.
Juan. María Rosa. Marcelino. Joaquina —
Joaquina with the little apple breasts.
You come laughing from the phone
announcing more people on the way:
I remember you running,
the dull plop of your body hitting water.

And also those nights of wild abandon
in the spacious house, all to ourselves
like some deserted convent,
and the longing for hidden doors,
that racing through rooms,
ransacking closets
and the thrill of alternately
dressing up and stripping down, dusting off
smoking jackets, top boots and trousers,
staging whimsical shows,

viejos sueños eróticos de nuestra adolescencia,
muchacho solitario.

                    Te acuerdas de Carmina,
de la gorda Carmina subiendo la escalera
con el culo en pompa
y llevando en la mano un candelabro?

Fue un verano feliz.

                    . . . *El último verano*
de nuestra juventud, dijiste a Juan
en Barcelona al regresar
nostálgicos,
y tenías razón. Luego vino el invierno,
el infierno de meses
y meses de agonía
y la noche final de pastillas y alcohol
y vómito en la alfombra.

                    Yo me salvé escribiendo
después de la muerte de Jaime Gil de Biedma.

De los dos, eras tú quien mejor escribía.
Ahora sé hasta qué punto tuyos eran
el deseo de ensueño y la ironía,
la sordina romántica que late en los poemas
míos que yo prefiero, por ejemplo en *Pandémica* . . .
A veces me pregunto
cómo será sin ti mi poesía.

Aunque acaso fui yo quien te enseñó.
Quien te enseñó a vengarte de mis sueños,
por cobardía, corrompiéndolos.

old sexual fantasies from our adolescence,
lonely little boy.
                    Remember Carmina,
big fat Carmina climbing up the stairs
with her ass sticking out
and a candelabra in her hand?

It was a wonderful summer . . .
                    "The last summer
of our youth," as you told Juan
when you went back to Barcelona,
both so nostalgic,
and you were right. Later came winter,
the hell of month
after month of agony
and the final night of pills and booze
and vomit on the carpet.
                    I saved my skin writing
after the death of Jaime Gil de Biedma.

Of the two, you were the better writer.
Now I know to what degree the craving
for fantasy and irony were yours,
the muted romanticism pulsing in poems
of mine I like best, like "Pandemic and Celeste."
Sometimes I ask myself what
my poetry will be like without you.

Though maybe I was the one who taught you.
Taught you to get even with my dreams,
dragging them down into the dirt. You coward.

ARTES DE SER MADURO

A José Antonio

Todavía la vieja tentación
de los cuerpos felices y de la juventud
tiene atractivo para mí,
no me deja dormir
y esta noche me excita.

Porque alguien contó historias
de pescadores en la playa,
cuando vuelven: la raya del amanecer
marcando, lívida, el límite del mar,
y asan sardinas frescas
en espetones, sobre la arena.
Lo imagino en seguida.
Y me coge un deseo de vivir
y ver amanecer, acostándome tarde,
que no está en proporción con la edad que ya tengo.

Aunque quizás alivie despertarse
a otro ritmo, mañana.
                    Liberado
de las exaltaciones de esta noche,
de sus fantasmas en *blue jeans.*

Como libros leídos han pasado los años
que van quedando lejos, ya sin razón de ser
— obras de otro momento.
                    Y el ansia de llorar
y el roce de la sábana, que me tenía inquieto
en las odiosas noches de verano,
el lujo de impaciencia y el don de la elegía
y el don de disciplina aplicada al ensueño,
mi fe en la gran historia . . .
Soldado de la guerra perdida de la vida,
mataron mi caballo, casi no lo recuerdo.
Hasta que me estremece
un ramalazo de sensualidad.

Envejecer tiene su gracia.
Es igual que de joven
aprender a bailar, plegarse a un ritmo
más insistente que nuestra inexperiencia.
Y procura también cierto instintivo
placer curioso,
una segunda naturaleza.

ARTS OF GROWING OLD

To José Antonio

Yet still I'm drawn
to that old temptation
of exuberant bodies, of youth,
that won't let me sleep
and gets me going tonight.

All because of stories someone told
about fishermen on the beach
when they dock: dawn streaking
a bruise along the sea's outline
as they roast fresh sardines
on spits in the sand.
In a flash I can picture it.
And all out of proportion to how old I am,
I'm seized by the urge to live, to stay up
all night to watch day break.

Though maybe it'd help to wake
tomorrow to a new rythm.
                              Freed
from tonight's raptures,
its blue-jeaned ghosts.

Just like books already read seem meaningless now,
weathered by years left farther and farther behind —
closed books of another time.
                              Like longing to weep
and the itchy sheet that kept me tossing
during spiteful summer nights.
And the luxury of impatience and talent for elegy
and ability to submit fantasy to form,
my faith in history's greatness . . . .
A soldier in life's battle lost,
I barely remember, they shot my horse.
Until a whiplash of lust
makes me tremble.

Growing old can be graceful.
It's like learning to dance
when young, giving in to a rhythm
more insistent than steps you don't know.
And it also breeds a certain
strange and spontaneous pleasure.
A second nature.

HIMNO A LA JUVENTUD

Heu quantum per se candida forma valet!

– Propercio, II, xxix, 30

A qué vienes ahora,
juventud,
encanto descarado de la vida?
Qué te trae a la playa?
Estábamos tranquilos los mayores
y tú vienes a herirnos, reviviendo
los más temibles sueños imposibles,
tú vienes para hurgarnos las imaginaciones.

De las ondas surgida,
toda brillos, fulgor, sensación pura
y ondulaciones de animal latente,
hacia la orilla avanzas
con sonrosados pechos diminutos,
con nalgas maliciosas lo mismo que sonrisas,
oh diosa esbelta de tobillos gruesos,
y con la insinuación
(tan propiamente tuya)
del vientre dando paso al nacimiento
de los muslos: belleza delicada,
precisa e indecisa,
donde posar la frente derramando lágrimas.

Y te vemos llegar — figuración
de un fabuloso espacio ribereño
con toros, caracolas y delfines,
sobre la arena blanda, entre la mar y el cielo,
aún trémula de gotas,
deslumbrada de sol y sonriendo.

Nos anuncias el reino de la vida,
el sueño de otra vida, más intensa y más libre,
sin deseo enconado como un remordimiento
— sin deseo de ti, sofisticada
bestezuela infantil, en quien coinciden
la directa belleza de la *starlet*
y la graciosa timidez del príncipe.

Aunque de pronto frunzas
la frente que atormenta un pensamiento
conmovedor y obtuso,
y volviendo hacia el mar tu rostro donde brilla

HYMN TO YOUTH

Heu quantum per se candida forma valet!

– Propertius, II, xxix, 30

What are you up to now,
youth,
life's bratty siren?
What brings you to this beach?
Here we grown-ups were in peace
and along you come to hurt us,
dredging up the most dreadful,
impossible dreams, along you come
to stir our imaginations.

Rising from ripples,
all sparkles, glimmer, sheer feeling
and undulations of the animal inside,
you wade toward shore
with blushing rosebud breasts,
with buttocks malicious as smiles,
oh thick-ankled, svelte goddess,
and with the innuendo
(so much your own)
of your belly tappering into the birth
of your thighs: fragile beauty,
chiseled and hesitant,
a place to rest the forehead, weeping.

And we see you emerge — decoration
from some fabulous riverbank scene
with bulls, conch-horns and dolphins —
across soft sand, between sea and sky,
still shimmering with drops,
dazzled by sun and smiling.

You herald the kingdom of life to us,
the dream of a freer one, more intense,
without desire festering like regret —
and without desiring you, worldly
childlike little creature
in whom the starlet's spotlit beauty
blends with the prince's bashful grace.

Even though your forehead
suddenly furrows, perturbed
by some vaguely disturbing thought,
and your face turns back to the sea

entre mojadas mechas rubias
la expresión melancólica de Antínoos,
oh bella indiferente,
por la playa camines como si no supieses
que te siguen los hombres y los perros,
los dioses y los ángeles,
y los arcángeles,
los tronos, las abominaciones . . .

glistening among wet blond strands
with the melancholy gaze of Antinous,
you stroll down the beach,
oh cold beauty, as if you didn't know
men and dogs are following you,
gods and angels,
archangels,
thrones, abominations . . . .

DE VITA BEATA

En un viejo país ineficiente,
algo así como España entre dos guerras
civiles, en un pueblo junto al mar,
poseer una casa y poca hacienda
y memoria ninguna. No leer,
no sufrir, no escribir, no pagar cuentas,
y vivir como un noble arruinado
entre las ruinas de mi inteligencia.

DE VITA BEATA

In an antique land where nothing works,
something like Spain between two civil
wars, in a village next to the sea,
here with a house and few possessions
and no memory at all: neither reading,
suffering, writing nor paying bills,
and living on like a bankrupt count
among the ruins of my intelligence.

These notes are to clarify aspects of Spanish culture important to the poems, translate quotations from other languages and give some pertinent background. Books that have been useful in preparing the introduction and notes are:

Cañas, Dionisio, ed. *Volver*. Madrid: Cátedra, 1990.
García Hortelano, Juan, ed. *El grupo poético de los años 50:*
    una antología. Madrid: Taurus Ediciones, 1978.
Gil de Biedma, Jaime. *Retrato del artista en 1956*. Barcelona:
    Editorial Lumen, 1991.
Mangini, Shirley. *Gil de Biedma*. Madrid: Ediciones Júcar, 1977.
Rovira, Pere. *La poesía de Jaime Gil de Biedma*. Barcelona:
    Edicions del Mall, 1986.

*

Great Expectations: The epigraph means "the dead seize the moment." This poem is based on Gil de Biedma's early experiences working at the Philippine Tobacco Company, where his father was a director.

From Now On: The title of the first volume, *Compañeros de viaje*, refers to the artists, labor leaders and intellectuals who formed the underground resistance to Franco. Not all of them, however, were "fellow travelers" of the Communist Party, the exclusive American meaning of this term. The poem describes Gil de Biedma's moment of commitment to resistance solidarity.

Homeless Ghosts: An *aparecido* is a displaced soul that returns to wander among the living, compared here to the poor and suffering who haunted Spanish streets during the long post-Civil War era.

Piazza del Popolo: In the spring of 1956, on his way home from Manila, Gil de Biedma stopped off in Rome to visit the exiled Spanish philosopher-poet María Zambrano, a disciple of Ortega y Gasset and a central figure in the Republican literary world. At that time she lived at number 3, Piazza del Popolo (Plaza of the People). Of this meeting, Gil de Biedma writes that "she spoke of our war, the final exodus, of her emotion on hearing a multitude sing 'The Internationale' in the Piazza del Popolo, with such vivacity, with such an intensity that I felt ennobled, exhalted to a great height, purified of all trivial desires. When I left her . . . I wrote twenty lines, the monster of a poem that I'd like to write, telling what she told me" (*Retrato*, p. 122).

In the Name of Today: This dedicatory poem to *Morality Plays* mentions by first name the "social poets" of the 50's Generation in this order: Carlos Barral, Ángel González, Alfonso Costafreda, (Pepe) José Ángel Valente, Gabriel Celaya, Gabriel Ferrater, Pepe Caballero Bonald, Miguel Barceló, José Agustín Goytisolo and Blas de Otero.

Barcelona Ja No És Bona, or My Solitary Spring Walk: The title alludes to a popular Catalan expression, "Barcelona és bona si la bossa sona" (Barcelona's good if your pocketbook's full) by beginning with a phrase that means "Barcelona's no good any more." The poem narrates a walk through Montjuic, a hillside park bordering Barcelona, site of the International Exhibition in 1929 (and the 1992 Olympics). The Exhibition marked the pre-Civil War apogee of the *cultureta*, or the educated Catalan upper-middle class. On one hand, they demonstrated their good taste by commissioning modernist artists such as Gaudí to beautify the city and, on the other, were mostly factory owners who exploited Southern immigrant labor from Andalusia and Murcia. This bourgeoisie had their summer mansions, as mentioned in the poem, in the nearby seaside towns of Sitges and Caldetas.

Sad October Night, 1959: This was written shortly before the largest general strike in Spain since the Civil War. The public protest movement, infiltrating like rain, is hinted at in the last line by "Letras protestadas," a legal term for defaulted payments. Both meanings are included in the translation.

From Here to Eternity: The title echoes the American war novel by James Jones and the saying "De Madrid al cielo," or "First Madrid then to heaven." The epigraph is from a popular *zarzuela*, or musical comedy song. Spanish nativity scenes are detailed dioramas depicting the Bethlehem hillsides on a grand scale. Entering Franco's capitol the car, of course, turns to the right.

Days in Pagsanjan: Pagsanjan is a scenic town located forty miles southeast of Manila, famous for its waterfall and male prostitution. *Apocalpyse Now* was filmed there.

Queen: Although literally "crazy woman," in street argot *loca* means an effeminate homosexual. Gil de Biedma has pointed out that the personality traits of the *loca* are a "passionate sociocultural product of the ghetto [which] can swing between grotesque parody and the stylized irony of the 'faggot.' By ironically assuming the false image others have created for him, the homosexual is trying to show that he has accepted himself, along with all of the consequences" (Cañas, p. 145).

Tale of a Poor Young Man: The title is from a popular Spanish movie of the 1940's based on Octave Feuillet's *Le roman d'un jeune homme pauve*. Santa Rita is a town in Pampagana, a rural province in Luzon. Isaac Peral Street is in Manila's red light district.

In Luna Castle: *The Romancer of Bernardo del Carpio* tells of the legendary Spanish folk hero who believed himself to be the son of King Alfonso II of Leon, although Alfonso had imprisoned his real father for a lifetime in Luna Castle. When Bernardo learned the truth and demanded his father's release, the king delivered him as a blinded cadaver riding a horse. Gil de Biedma uses this legend to parallel the fate of his orphaned generation, receiving their true "fathers" after lunar imprisonments in Franco's jails. The second-to-last line, "que nuestra España de todos," is an echo of Francoist propaganda and, to give the ending the same ironic punch in English, I've substituded a phrase of American rhetoric.

All Saints Day: The *día de difuntos* is a holiday the day after American Halloween when, in Catholic cultures, people visit family tombs to honor the dead. In Spain, those who have died as good Catholics are buried in the sacramental cemeteries, often belonging to religious brotherhoods. Anticlerical Republican leaders such as Pablo Iglesias, however, were buried apart from the rest.

Ruins of the Third Reich: This is a parody of "Lili Marlene," a German love song that inspired the troops during World War II. In this version the soldier boyfriend lies defeated on the front, imagining what has become of his patriotic sweetheart with the fall of the Third Reich. "Wie einst," a phrase from the song, means "like then."

Elegy in Memory of the French Song: The epigraph is from the song known in English as "Autumn Leaves": "It's a song / so much like us." The poem follows the song in several ways and quotes a phrase, "sans faire de bruit," or "without making any noise."

Pandemic and Celeste: (a) The title refers to the two Aphrodites mentioned in the *Symposium*, symbolizing promiscuous and monagamous love. (b) Catullus, in poem VII, considers Lesbia's question: "You ask how many of your kisses, Lesbia, would be enough for me?" The answer is quoted here in the epigraph: "As numerous as the sands of Libya . . . or as the stars, when night is quiet, which contemplate the furtive loves of men." (c) The first stanza quotes from Baudelaire's "To the Reader": "my likeness — my brother." (d) "The poet" of the third stanza is John Donne, paraphrased from "The Ecstasy." (e) The fourth stanza quotes from Mallarmé's "The Afternoon of a Fawn": "of the languor poorly savored between two people." (f) In English it is impossible to keep the ambiguous gender of the *su* referring to the lover in the final stanzas. The choice should

113

clearly be "his," although in Gil de Biedma's love poetry the homoeroticism is never explicit.

Nostalgie de la Boue: The title is Baudelairean and means a longing for the lowlife.

After the Death of Jaime Gil de Biedma: About this poem Gil de Biedma said that "I wrote it in July of 1966. I was afraid of finding myself a suicide before I could react. Therefore, it occured to me: create for myself the idea that I'd already gone through with it" (Cañas, p. 150). The scene is set at the family house in Nava de la Asunción, Segovia.

Hymn to Youth: The epigraph translates as "How much your brillant form itself stands out." The poem is based on Baudelaire's "Hymn to Beauty." Antinous, the favorite male lover of the Roman emperor Hadrian, drowned in the Nile and his image was then made into a famous symbol of youthful beauty. At the end the poem plays with the nine celestial orders in medieval angelology, which from the top are: seraphim, cherubim, thrones, dominations . . . .

De Vita Beata: The title is a Latin expression that means a pious retirement from life. From this comes the Spanish meaning for *beata:* an elderly woman dressed in black who haunts the churches.

CITY LIGHTS PUBLICATIONS

Allen, Roberta. AMAZON DREAM
Angulo de, Jaime. INDIANS IN OVERALLS
Angulo de, G. & J. JAIME IN TAOS
Artaud, Antonin. ARTAUD ANTHOLOGY
Bataille, Georges. EROTISM: Death and Sensuality
Bataille, Georges. THE IMPOSSIBLE
Bataille, Georges. STORY OF THE EYE
Bataille, Georges. THE TEARS OF EROS
Baudelaire, Charles. INTIMATE JOURNALS
Baudelaire, Charles. TWENTY PROSE POEMS
Bowles, Paul. A HUNDRED CAMELS IN THE COURTYARD
Broughton, James. MAKING LIGHT OF IT
Brown, Rebecca. ANNIE OAKLEY'S GIRL
Brown, Rebecca. THE TERRIBLE GIRLS
Bukowski, Charles. THE MOST BEAUTIFUL WOMAN IN TOWN
Bukowski, Charles. NOTES OF A DIRTY OLD MAN
Bukowski, Charles. TALES OF ORDINARY MADNESS
Burroughs, William S. THE BURROUGHS FILE
Burroughs, William S. THE YAGE LETTERS
Cassady, Neal. THE FIRST THIRD
Choukri, Mohamed. FOR BREAD ALONE
CITY LIGHTS REVIEW #2: AIDS & the Arts
CITY LIGHTS REVIEW #3: Media and Propaganda
CITY LIGHTS REVIEW #4: Literature / Politics / Ecology
Cocteau, Jean. THE WHITE BOOK (LE LIVRE BLANC)
Codrescu, Andrei, ed. EXQUISITE CORPSE READER
Cornford, Adam. ANIMATIONS
Corso, Gregory. GASOLINE
Daumal, René. THE POWERS OF THE WORD
David-Neel, Alexandra. SECRET ORAL TEACHINGS IN TIBETAN BUDDHIST SECTS
Deleuze, Gilles. SPINOZA: Practical Philosophy
Dick, Leslie. WITHOUT FALLING
di Prima, Diane. PIECES OF A SONG: Selected Poems
Doolittle, Hilda (H.D.) NOTES ON THOUGHT & VISION
Ducornet, Rikki. ENTERING FIRE
Duras, Marguerite. DURAS BY DURAS
Eidus, Janice. VITO LOVES GERALDINE
Eberhardt, Isabelle. THE OBLIVION SEEKERS
Fenollosa, Ernest. CHINESE WRITTEN CHARACTER AS A MEDIUM FOR POETRY
Ferlinghetti, Lawrence. PICTURES OF THE GONE WORLD
Ferlinghetti, Lawrence. SEVEN DAYS IN NICARAGUA LIBRE
Finley, Karen. SHOCK TREATMENT
Ford, Charles Henri. OUT OF THE LABYRINTH: Selected Poems
Franzen, Cola, transl. POEMS OF ARAB ANDALUSIA
García Lorca, Federico. BARBAROUS NIGHTS: Legends & Plays
García Lorca, Federico. ODE TO WALT WHITMAN & OTHER POEMS
García Lorca, Federico. POEM OF THE DEEP SONG
Gil de Biedma, Jaime. LONGING: SELECTED POEMS
Ginsberg, Allen. HOWL & OTHER POEMS
Ginsberg, Allen. KADDISH & OTHER POEMS
Ginsberg, Allen. REALITY SANDWICHES
Ginsberg, Allen. PLANET NEWS
Ginsberg, Allen. THE FALL OF AMERICA
Ginsberg, Allen. MIND BREATHS
Ginsberg, Allen. PLUTONIAN ODE
Goethe, J. W. von. TALES FOR TRANSFORMATION
Hayton-Keeva, Sally, ed. VALIANT WOMEN IN WAR AND EXILE
Herron, Don. THE DASHIELL HAMMETT TOUR: A Guidebook

Herron, Don. THE LITERARY WORLD OF SAN FRANCISCO
Higman, Perry, tr. LOVE POEMS FROM SPAIN AND SPANISH AMERICA
Jaffe, Harold. EROS: ANTI-EROS
Jenkins, Edith. AGAINST A FIELD SINISTER
Kerouac, Jack. BOOK OF DREAMS
Kerouac, Jack. POMES ALL SIZES
Kerouac, Jack. SCATTERED POEMS
Lacarrière, Jacques. THE GNOSTICS
La Duke, Betty. COMPANERAS
La Loca. ADVENTURES ON THE ISLE OF ADOLESCENCE
Lamantia, Philip. MEADOWLARK WEST
Laughlin, James. SELECTED POEMS: 1935-1985
Le Brun, Annie. SADE: On the Brink of the Abyss
Lowry, Malcolm. SELECTED POEMS
Mackey, Nathaniel. SCHOOL OF UDHRA
Marcelin, Philippe-Thoby. THE BEAST OF THE HAITIAN HILLS
Masereel, Frans. PASSIONATE JOURNEY
Mayakovsky, Vladimir. LISTEN! EARLY POEMS
Mrabet, Mohammed. THE BOY WHO SET THE FIRE
Mrabet, Mohammed. THE LEMON
Mrabet, Mohammed. LOVE WITH A FEW HAIRS
Mrabet, Mohammed. M'HASHISH
Murguía, A. & B. Paschke, eds. VOLCAN: Poems from Central America
Murillo, Rosario. ANGEL IN THE DELUGE
Paschke, B. & D. Volpendesta, eds. CLAMOR OF INNOCENCE
Pasolini, Pier Paolo. ROMAN POEMS
Pessoa, Fernando. ALWAYS ASTONISHED
Peters, Nancy J., ed. WAR AFTER WAR (City Lights Review #5)
Poe, Edgar Allan. THE UNKNOWN POE
Porta, Antonio. KISSES FROM ANOTHER DREAM
Prévert, Jacques. PAROLES
Purdy, James. THE CANDLES OF YOUR EYES
Purdy, James. IN A SHALLOW GRAVE
Purdy, James. GARMENTS THE LIVING WEAR
Rachlin, Nahid. MARRIED TO A STRANGER
Rachlin, Nahid. VEILS: SHORT STORIES
Rey Rosa, Rodrigo. THE BEGGAR'S KNIFE
Rey Rosa, Rodrigo. DUST ON HER TONGUE
Rigaud, Milo. SECRETS OF VOODOO
Ruy Sánchez, Alberto. MOGADOR
Saadawi El, Nawal. MEMOIRS OF A WOMAN DOCTOR
Sawyer-Lauçanno, Christopher, tr. THE DESTRUCTION OF THE JAGUAR
Sclauzero, Mariarosa. MARLENE
Serge, Victor. RESISTANCE
Shepard, Sam. MOTEL CHRONICLES
Shepard, Sam. FOOL FOR LOVE & THE SAD LAMENT OF PECOS BILL
Smith, Michael. IT A COME
Snyder, Gary. THE OLD WAYS
Solnit, Rebecca. SECRET EXHIBITION: Six California Artists
Sussler, Betsy, ed. BOMB: INTERVIEWS
Takahashi, Mutsuo. SLEEPING SINNING FALLING
Turyn, Anne, ed. TOP TOP STORIES
Tutuola, Amos. FEATHER WOMAN OF THE JUNGLE
Tutuola, Amos. SIMBI & THE SATYR OF THE DARK JUNGLE
Valaoritis, Nanos. MY AFTERLIFE GUARANTEED
Wilson, Colin. POETRY AND MYSTICISM
Wilson, Peter Lamborn. SACRED DRIFT
Zamora, Daisy. RIVERBED OF MEMORY